Strategic Intelligence
for American National Security

Strategic Intelligence
for American National Security

Bruce D. Berkowitz and Allan E. Goodman

PRINCETON UNIVERSITY PRESS

Princeton, New Jersey

Copyright © 1989 by Princeton University Press
Published by Princeton University Press,
41 William Street, Princeton, New Jersey 08540
In the United Kingdom:
Princeton University Press,
Guildford, Surrey

All Rights Reserved

Library of Congress Cataloging-in-Publication Data
Berkowitz, Bruce D., 1956-
Strategic intelligence for American national security
Bruce D. Berkowitz and Allan E. Goodman.
p. cm. Bibliography: p. Includes index.
ISBN 0-691-07805-X (alk. paper)
1. Military intelligence—United States.
2. United States—National security.
I. Goodman, Allan E., 1944-
II. Title.
UB251.U5B47 1989 335.3′432′0973—dc19 88-29326 CIP

This book has been composed in Linotron Baskerville

Clothbound editions of Princeton University Press books are
printed on acid-free paper, and binding materials are chosen
for strength and durability. Paperbacks, although satisfactory
for personal collections, are not usually suitable for library rebinding

Printed in the United States of America
by Princeton University Press,
Princeton, New Jersey

Contents

List of Figures

Preface

Strategic intelligence is many things: a mission, a skill, a national capability. In addition to all of this, however, strategic intelligence is also a matter of public policy, and, like most other policy issues, it can be discussed intelligently by the general public. Indeed, such discussions are necessary to develop an effective intelligence policy and one that meets the requirements of U.S. officials and the expectations of the American public.

This book outlines some of the issues that the U.S. intelligence community faces today and the challenges that it will need to face in the future. Many of them are traditional problems, such as how to do analysis or deciding what kinds of information intelligence consumers require. Others are a result of having to operate a large, complex organization effectively. Yet others are the result of changes in technology and society as a whole and changing political conditions. We have tried to describe some of these problems and, even more importantly, the choices that the U.S. intelligence community will have to make in order to respond to the needs of its consumers.

This book originally began several years ago as an update of Sherman Kent's classic text *Strategic Intelligence for American World Policy*, a book that was important in the development of the authors' own thinking about the problems of intelligence. Much has changed in the four decades that have passed since Kent first addressed the subject, however, and so the book that emerged from our efforts is not an update or revision of Kent's work so much as it is a book written for the same reasons but about different problems.

When Sherman Kent wrote *Strategic Intelligence*, the United

States had relatively little experience in intelligence; what understanding we did have was based mainly on our involvement in World War II. American leaders were sorting out the very basics about what intelligence was supposed to be and what an intelligence community was supposed to do. Today, on the other hand, we have almost forty years of experience in producing strategic intelligence and probably understand the basic principles better. Our expectations for intelligence and the demands we have placed on the intelligence community have also changed, and the political, technical, and economic environments are quite different today. So what we have written is the same kind of book as did Kent—an overview of the current problems of intelligence and an outline for addressing them—but one that deals with a number of new issues and the new ways traditional issues must be addressed.

Many books about intelligence have appeared lately, so it might be useful to make clear where this book fits into the field.

Many books written within the past few years try to describe in as much detail as possible how the intelligence community is organized and what its precise capabilities are. Aside from the fact that the information in these books cannot be confirmed (and is, in fact, often wrong or badly outdated), we frankly doubt that the best way to debate and develop U.S. policy for strategic intelligence is to reveal the names and location of CIA operatives or to provide the resolution of U.S. reconnaissance satellites to three decimal places. Indeed, since intelligence does require at least some amount of secrecy to protect sources and methods, it seems to us that if public discussions of intelligence amount only to compilations of leaked information then those critics who claim the discussion of intelligence is best left to a small group of elite specialists may have a point.

Effective intelligence does, unfortunately, require some restrictions on information, and these restrictions are sometimes inconsistent with the requirements of democracy. Some people believe that the operation of an effective intelligence agency is incompatible with democracy. We disagree. When detailed information is necessary for a debate over intelligence policy, a reasonable compromise between democracy and security is to debate the issues in secret in a small, but representative, group of officials (which, of course, is the intent of the oversight bodies in Congress and the executive branch).

Most basic intelligence issues, however, can be intelligently discussed like other public policy issues without violating requirements for secrecy. Detailed information that would, if disclosed, endanger sources and methods may be necessary for the day-to-day management of intelligence and decisions affecting specific intelligence systems, but it is not critical to formulating and evaluating intelligence policy itself.

For example, building a reconnaissance satellite obviously requires one to know the maximum focal length or antenna size that will fit on a satellite intended to be launched from a particular booster or to collect a particular type of data. But such details are no more critical to a public discussion of intelligence than, say, the precise specifications of a thermonuclear weapon are critical to a discussion of arms control or a graduate-level description of the biochemistry of DNA splicing is needed for a discussion of environmental safeguards in genetic engineering.

Other recent books on intelligence have been exposés of alleged wrongdoing on the part of U.S. intelligence organizations. These books have their place—especially when dealing with oversight issues, as in the case of the recent Iran-Contra affair—but, for the most part, exposés are less relevant for understanding strategic intelligence than for debating covert action or specific collection programs of dubious propriety or legality. Failures in strategic intelligence are usually more a matter of simple error or misfeasance, not malfeasance.

Yet, one might ask, why is it necessary to debate intelligence issues in public at all, even if it were possible to do so without compromising sources and methods? Why not just leave the subject to the experts in the intelligence community and the special committees that are cleared and designated to deal with such issues?

The answer is that intelligence is an issue that will be decided by the American political process, just as defense, retirement, health, housing, transportation, education, and many other issues will be. We would never dream of leaving all decisions affecting these issues to a select few. We might be willing to defer to the experts on specific technical questions, but most Americans would probably agree that a public debate on the broader topics within these issues is necessary if democratic government is to work as intended and if officials are to be responsive to the views of the people.

Like it or not, the effectiveness of U.S. intelligence depends on how it is treated by the American political process. If people are unaware of the factors that determine whether intelligence analysis is effective, how intelligence planning works, or what new developments will make intelligence more expensive and more difficult to produce, it is less likely that the American political system will respond with the resources necessary to meet the challenges. Any intelligence program can fail because it was poorly conceived or because it was compromised, but no intelligence program that lacked funding was ever successful. So, while many writers have questioned whether it is possible to discuss intelligence issues in public, we would put the issue another way: if a democratic government is to have an effective intelligence service, these issues *must* be discussed in public.

We have thus provided an outline of intelligence issues, identifying the problems to be solved and the choices to be made in the years ahead. The objective is to enable a person interested in national security issues to understand today's intelligence problems and to decide how they should be addressed. We have not tried to provide an exhaustive plan for reforming or improving the intelligence community so much as to lay out the major terms of reference for a discussion of intelligence policy.

This book would not have been possible without the cooperation of many people. Special thanks go to the intelligence officials and former officials who agreed to be interviewed for this book. (These individuals are listed by position in Appendix C.) Many of them provided comments on earlier drafts of the manuscript, for which we are grateful. During the writing of this book, we also benefited greatly from the comments and suggestions generously provided by Diana Furchtgott-Roth, Michael Hermann, C. William Maynes, Bernard F. McMahon, Paul Pillar, E. Steven Potts, John Prados, Rose Mary Sheldon, Dana Sutton, and George Thibault.

As individuals previously employed by the intelligence community who have certain voluntarily assumed legal responsibilities intended to protect intelligence sources and methods, we submitted the manuscript to the Publications Review Board at the Central Intelligence Agency and appreciated their expeditious review. Of course, this review does not constitute authentification or endorsement, and the views expressed here are solely those of the authors.

Finally, the authors would like to thank Sanford G. Thatcher, editor at Princeton University Press, who encouraged us to work together on this project and supported us throughout.

Strategic Intelligence
for American National Security

ONE

Strategic Intelligence Today

Nearly forty years ago a history professor at Yale University wrote a book that introduced a new term to the American lexicon of national security: "strategic intelligence."[1] The author, Sherman Kent, had served in the Analysis and Research Division of the Office of Strategic Services (OSS) during World War II and was about to leave academia to return to government service and help establish the American intelligence community that endures to this day.

Kent, like George Kennan, Dean Acheson, and many other thinkers in the U.S. foreign policy community at the time, believed that the United States was entering a new era in which it could no longer maintain its pre-World War II policy of isolationism. The traditional leader of the Western democracies, Great Britain, was exhausted after two world wars. Moreover, a new threat, it was said, had emerged. Many U.S. officials believed the Soviet Union was committed to a policy of, if not outright conquest, then at least determined expansion.

As a result, they concluded, the United States would have to protect its national interests throughout the world without the support of a stronger ally. It would also have to create and lead an international anti-Communist alliance and maintain a larger standing army. And, because of the peculiar nature of the Cold War, American leaders would have to learn the skills necessary for protecting U.S. interests in situations short of war but also short of true peace. A key requirement for American security in this new era, wrote Kent, was "strategic intelligence."

Strategic intelligence differs from traditional operational intelligence, or what the Duke of Wellington described as "knowing what was on the other side of the hill." Operational intelligence (also called "tactical intelligence") is knowledge about the immediate situation and is based almost entirely on straightforward observation—say, the number of tanks in the next village and their direction of movement. Strategic intelligence has a wider base and broader objective, integrating economics, politics, social studies, and the study of technology. Strategic intelligence is designed to provide officials with the "big picture" and long-range forecasts they need in order to plan for the future.

Strategic intelligence had been part of national security policy for almost as long as there have been nations, though some governments had mastered it better than others. In the ancient world, for example, the Carthaginians were especially skilled in developing intelligence on their adversaries, as were their forbearers, the Phoenicians and the other trading states of the eastern Mediterranean. The Romans were not.[2] In the modern world, the British were known throughout the world for their intelligence expertise, as were the Russians and their successors, the Soviets. The Americans, on the other hand, were not, and Kent believed that this was intolerable in the hazardous world of the latter half of the twentieth century.

Strategic Intelligence was probably the most influential book on intelligence analysis ever written. Not only did it become a standard text for American students of intelligence, it was also widely read abroad, eventually being published in French, Russian, German, and other languages. (According to one of his long-time associates, Kent, who had an ironic sense of humor, was especially fond of his copy of the Chinese edition—a pirated version made in Taiwan in violation of the copyright laws.)

Sherman Kent was himself to leave a lasting impression on U.S. intelligence that went well beyond his written work. A few months after *Strategic Intelligence* was published, Kent was recruited by Harvard historian William Langer to return to the government. Langer, who had been Chief of the Research and Analysis Division (R&A) of oss during the war, had been brought back into government service to overhaul the intelligence community's analytical arm in 1950. The community had recently committed two major intelligence blunders. First, it had failed to predict the invasion of South Korea in June 1950 by the North Koreans. Then it failed to predict that the new Communist regime in China would respond to Douglas MacArthur's approach to the Yalu River the following November by sending hundreds of thousands of troops across the border in a massive counterattack. This debacle resulted in the retreat of the United Nations forces back past the 38th parallel and one of the greatest setbacks to U.S. policy since World War II.

Director of Central Intelligence Walter Bedell ("Beedle") Smith was determined such failures would not be repeated, and so he instructed Langer to create a new unit responsible for comprehensive, forward-looking intelligence assessments. These assessments became known as National Intelligence Estimates (NIEs), and the organization Langer established became the Office of National Estimates (ONE). Langer became its first director, and he hired Kent as his deputy. When Langer returned to Harvard in 1952, Kent became director. He held the post for the next sixteen years. Needless to say, ONE and the process of developing NIEs bore a strong resemblance to the principles for analysis Kent described in *Strategic Intelligence*.[3]

This book, while not strictly speaking a sequel or an update of Kent's treatise, is written in much the same spirit. The purpose is to describe principles for producing effective intelligence. These principles cover a range of issues: planning intelligence, developing systems and methods to collect information, carrying out analysis, managing organizations. Also, the intelligence mission is likely to become much more challenging in the next few years, so this study discusses how the community can meet these challenges.

In this chapter, we briefly review the development of the U.S. intelligence community in order to explain the development of the problems the community faces today and to put these challenges into context. As we shall see, in many re-

spects the strategic intelligence mission is at least as critical—
if not more so—than when Sherman Kent wrote his book,
and possibly more difficult than ever.*

THE EVOLUTION OF THE MODERN U.S.
INTELLIGENCE COMMUNITY

Many different factors have shaped the structure and division of responsibilities in the U.S. intelligence community, so
it is understandable if the community lacks a clear-cut ge-
nealogy. Even so, it is still possible to sketch a general outline
of how the intelligence community came to assume its current form.

Strategic intelligence as we know it today—that is, analysis
produced in a process clearly separate from that used to develop policy, based on combined sources of information, and
intended to go beyond simple descriptions of military deployments or political events—hardly existed in the United States
before World War II. True, there was probably always someone in the national security bureaucracy concerned with current facts and future trends. But political analysis was traditionally contained in consular reports written by foreign
service officers. Most U.S. intelligence dealt strictly with military affairs. This intelligence was produced by the armed services: the Office of Naval Intelligence (ONI), established in
1882 by the Department of the Navy, and the Division for
Military Intelligence (MI), created by the War Department
three years later.

The armed services concentrated on information about the
numbers and capabilities of the weapons deployed by foreign
powers, reflecting the concern military leaders had to keep
up to date with the rapid development of military technology
that accompanied the Industrial Revolution. Even so, both
ONI and MI were minor operations caught in the backwaters
of the military bureaucracy. Neither consisted of more than

* After many years of public service, Sherman Kent died in late 1986.

three hundred officers before World War II, and neither had a unit solely dedicated to analysis.[4] Moreover, intelligence had a certain stigma in those days. Most officers in the 1800s believed that military skills decided—and, indeed, *should* decide—the outcome of battles and that using information about the enemy's weaknesses was "unfair," especially if this information was obtained clandestinely. So intelligence was a "less than honorable" profession; certainly no intelligence specialist could hope to rise to the top of his service. Indeed, the chief prerequisite for intelligence officers in those days may have been personal wealth, as attachés often had to cover their own travel and living expenses. Cutting the funding for attachés alleged to be "vacationing abroad at public expense" was a common practice for Congress until World War II.

Given this attitude, it is not surprising that the U.S. intelligence community developed only through a fit of starts and stops until World War II. The first civilian intelligence agency appears to have been the "secret service" operated for the Union forces during the Civil War by Allan Pinkerton, a private detective hired under contract. The Pinkerton Agency was mainly concerned with counterintelligence, or catching spies, rather than with "positive" intelligence, or estimating enemy forces. The Pinkerton Agency was disbanded at the end of the war, and intelligence was again left exclusively to the military services.

The next attempt at a civilian intelligence service was the State Department's Cipher Bureau, better known as the "American Black Chamber," which was operated by Herbert Yardley from 1917 to 1929. The Cipher Bureau was the first U.S. agency responsible for collecting, deciphering, and analyzing signals intelligence, or, as it is usually called today, SIGINT. The Cipher Bureau's mission was to intercept and decipher foreign diplomatic cables. By most accounts the bureau was effective—its greatest coup was the interception of Japanese diplomatic messages during the Washington Naval Conference—but it was dismantled by Secretary of State Henry Stimson, who thought such an operation violated the rules of international statesmanship. The remnants of the Cipher Bureau were transferred to the military, which had been developing its own tactical SIGINT operations for some time.[5]

Thus, by 1940, the United States had a minimal intelligence apparatus, most of which was concentrated in the military services. All of this was to change as a result of World War II, which was to produce a rapid expansion of the U.S. intelligence system. The war also led to the creation of the first civilian organization responsible for producing strategic intelligence, the Office of Strategic Services, or OSS. The OSS, which is usually cited as the predecessor of today's CIA, was established by presidential order on July 11, 1942. William J. Donovan, a World War I hero and nationally known lawyer, was appointed its first director.

One interesting fact histories of U.S. intelligence often overlook is that the analytic component of the CIA's predecessor was created before the clandestine collection and covert operation components. Even before the OSS was officially established Donovan organized a secret research office under the auspices of the Library of Congress in early 1941. This office was reorganized as the Research and Analysis Division of the OSS and ultimately provided the model for the CIA's current Directorate of Intelligence. The clandestine services components of the OSS—the predecessor of the CIA's current Directorate of Operations—were created several months later.[6]

Donovan lobbied in the closing months of World War II for preserving the OSS, but President Truman was suspicious of a civilian intelligence agency. Truman believed such an organization carried the potential for abuse and smacked of a "secret police." Donovan was also undone by some well-timed leaks of his proposals to the press by his opponents in Congress, the State Department, and the armed services, who did not want the intelligence mission taken over by a competitor. Consequently, following World War II intelligence reverted back to its prewar form: political matters were the responsibility of the State Department, and military intelligence (including collection of technical intelligence) was the responsibility of the armed services. The FBI was responsible for intelligence operations in Latin America, reflecting J. Edgar Hoover's persistent ambition to add foreign intelligence to the FBI's portfolio.[7]

After the OSS was divided among the State Department and the armed services, President Truman established a Central Intelligence Group (CIG). The CIG was supposed to oversee the coordination of intelligence and its dissemination within the executive branch, but it was not an independent agency. Rather, it was comprised of State, Army, and Navy personnel, and as one might expect from an organization out of the bureaucratic mainstream and lacking a budget of its own, the CIG proved virtually irrelevant. The most significant result of the creation of the CIG was that when the group was established so was the office of the Director of Central Intelligence (DCI).[8]

The onset of the Cold War, followed by a series of intelligence failures (some real, some perceived), led President Truman to change his mind about the wisdom of a strong centralized intelligence community. Under his initiative, the National Security Act of 1947, the law that created the basic structure of the U.S. national security establishment we know today, also established the legal basis for the modern intelligence community. The National Security Act created the Central Intelligence Agency and elevated the office of the DCI from a post established by executive directive to one with a basis in statutory law.

The provisions of the National Security Act listed four functions for the CIA:

— to advise the NSC on matters related to national security (this became the CIA's analysis function);

— to make recommendations to the NSC regarding the coordination of the intelligence activities of the departments (this became the basis for the authority of the DCI to direct and manage the entire national intelligence community);

— to correlate and evaluate intelligence and provide for its appropriate dissemination (this gave the CIA the lead in drafting NIEs and other community intelligence products); and

— to perform "other functions . . . as the NSC will from time to time direct" (this catch-all phrase was later used to authorize covert action operations).[9]

The CIA was further strengthened by the Central Intelligence Agency Act of 1949. Like most laws, however, the National Security Act and CIA Act required a dynamic official to flesh out the bare bones of the statutory language. The dynamic official in this case was the fourth DCI to hold office, Walter Bedell Smith. In addition to promoting CIA analysis within the executive branch, Smith established the Board of National Estimates (BNE) and the National Intelligence Estimates in 1950. The BNE used a CIA component, the Office of National Estimates, to draft and coordinate the estimates, and this enabled the CIA to have a pivotal role in the production of national strategic intelligence.

The analytical components of the CIA evolved throughout the 1950s and 1960s. Originally these components included the Office of Reports and Estimates (ORE), the Office of Scientific Intelligence (OSI), and the Office of Collection and Dissemination (OCD). In 1952 these offices were collected into a single unit, which later became known as the Directorate of Intelligence (DDI).[10] The CIA increased its capabilities for producing strategic estimates throughout the 1950s and 1960s, and the agency's status grew within the U.S. national security community.

Meanwhile, the analytical organizations within the Department of Defense were also evolving. Many of the offices responsible for analysis were consolidated into the Defense Intelligence Agency (DIA) in 1962. One reason for creating the DIA was to make military intelligence more responsive to the requirements of the Secretary of Defense and Joint Chiefs, though some former officials believe that an additional motive was to reduce the influence of the individual armed services in the production of intelligence estimates.

In either case, DIA required a number of years before it became a fully effective service. At least at first, contrary to the aphorism, the sum of the military intelligence offices was actually less than the total of the individual parts. Also, once DIA was created, the chiefs of the services' intelligence agencies were dropped both from the U.S. Intelligence Board and from voting participation in the drafting of NIEs, and though the chiefs were retained as consulting participants, this also helped establish CIA as the most important voice in national intelligence.[11] This situation was to continue until the early 1970s, when several factors combined to reduce the influence of the CIA in national intelligence assessments.

One factor was the realization that throughout the 1970s U.S. intelligence had underestimated Soviet military deployments in general and forecasts of Soviet strategic forces in particular.[12] A second factor was the style of Henry Kissinger, Assistant to the President for National Security in the early Nixon years, and later Secretary of State. Kissinger relied heavily on his own NSC staff for analysis. He also pressed the BNE to include more raw data in the NIEs. This enabled readers to extract their own conclusions and diluted the impact of the NIE itself.[13] A third factor was the measures for improvement that were undertaken by the military intelligence agencies. Secretary of Defense Melvin Laird and a succession of reform-minded DIA directors improved the quality and sophistication of DIA intelligence by bringing in a new generation of younger, better-trained analysts.

At the same time the other intelligence organizations were improving their capabilities, the BNE and ONE were losing much of their own continuity, as stalwarts who had worked on the NIE from the 1950s retired or left for other assignments. This was the period, for example, when Sherman Kent himself cut back his participation in intelligence affairs. Thus, when in 1973 several positions on the Board of National Estimates became vacant, DCI William Colby used the opportunity to abolish the BNE altogether, along with its supporting staff, ONE (in fact, much of the responsibility for drafting NIEs had already been passed to line offices in the DDI a few years earlier). In place of the BNE, Colby established a panel of National Intelligence Officers (NIOs), each with a particular area of expertise. For example, one NIO was appointed for Soviet strategic forces, another for Soviet conventional forces, another for Far Eastern affairs, and so on. The NIOs assumed responsibility for the production of NIEs but were not assigned a permanent staff. The staff work for NIEs was parceled out to offices within CIA, DIA, and other analytical offices in the community.[14]

One other factor that contributed to the decline of the stature of U.S. intelligence was money. After the Vietnam War, the CIA—along with the Defense Department and other members of the intelligence community—suffered a series of budget cuts. The effect of these cuts was magnified by the high rates of inflation prevailing at the time and the rapidly growing costs of technical collection systems, and it probably also lowered the morale of many intelligence officers.

By 1976, U.S. intelligence analysis—and especially the strategic estimates—had lost much of its stature. The community continued to produce NIEs and other intelligence assessments, but the influence of these products had diminished. Stansfield Turner, who assumed office as DCI in 1977, attempted to reverse this decline. Turner was only partly successful, however. The intelligence budget continued to suffer during much of his tenure, and since Turner was not considered a member of the inner circle of the Carter administration, the views contained in the estimates provided by the DCI were sometimes ignored.[15]

The first years of the Reagan administration were marked by the resurgence of CIA influence in policy-making circles and an increase in the stature of the intelligence community as a whole. Part of this was due to William Casey's close ties to the President, ties which insured that when the DCI presented the intelligence community's perspective, it would have influence at the top levels of the administration. Another reason was that intelligence budgets, which had begun to rise in the last years of the Carter administration, continued to grow substantially. The NIEs were reestablished as the premier product of the community, as Casey and his staff focused more of their efforts on them. The number of NIEs produced by the community roughly doubled during this period.[16] Nevertheless, the CIA and the NIEs would not regain the preeminence they enjoyed in the 1950s and early 1960s. By 1980, the DIA and other members of the community had established themselves as full players, and it was not possible to reverse this. Today, as the accompanying diagram shows, every agency that is engaged in the formulation or implementation of foreign policy has an intelligence arm.

The key problems for the analytical elements of the U.S. intelligence community in the closing years of the Reagan administration appeared to be partly fiscal and partly political. By 1985, the defense buildup started in the late 1970s had stalled, and defense budgets started to decline. As we

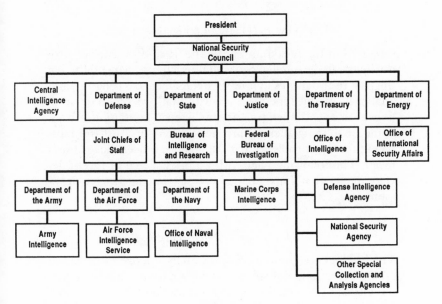

FIGURE 1.1
U.S. Intelligence Agencies

shall see, intelligence spending has historically been closely correlated with defense spending, so the issue arose as to whether the intelligence community would suffer the same kinds of spending cuts as would defense and whether such cuts would undermine U.S. intelligence capabilities. Meanwhile, on the political front, the Iran-Contra arms affair raised questions concerning the integrity of certain U.S. intelligence officials, the effectiveness of oversight over the intelligence community's operations, and even the objectivity of its analysts. Although the scandal occurred over an illegally conducted covert action, the analytic components of the intelligence community were also dragged into the controversy at some points when it became known that some top officials had selectively used intelligence analysis to promote the ill-conceived operation. For a time, "Irangate" appeared likely to discredit even those officials and parts of the intelligence community that played little or no part in the affair.[17]

THE NEW INTELLIGENCE ENVIRONMENT

One reason for reexamining the theory and practice of producing strategic intelligence is that much has changed during the past four decades in how such intelligence is collected and analyzed, in the types of products that are required, and, hence, in the challenges the intelligence community faces. Some of these challenges are new; others are just the most recent form of problems that intelligence officers have always faced. The following pages offer a brief sketch of recent developments that have shaped today's intelligence environment.

The Multiplication of Targets

The intelligence community must analyze more information on a greater range of subjects today than ever before. When the Office of National Estimates was established, it consisted of just four divisions: Western Europe, Eastern Europe and the Soviet Union, the Far East, and the Middle East. Each division had just two to four analysts. Yet this organization was sufficient to produce all of the National Intelligence Estimates' top U.S. policymakers required at the time.[18] Though ONE admittedly relied on the rest of the Central Intelligence Agency, the State Department, and the military intelligence services for basic research, the simplicity of its structure nevertheless reflected the world situation in the late 1940s and early 1950s. Most territories of Africa and Asia were still colonies and did not pose significant threats to American national security. The intelligence world that ONE had to analyze was also much less technical and much less specialized than today.

Now, of course, these conditions have changed. Rather than the 51 countries that originally comprised the United Nations, 159 countries belong to the organization today. This simple fact alone reflects an intelligence problem: now there are many more countries whose activities must be monitored and more officials for whom biographical files must be collected. For the intelligence community there is simply more politics in the world to cover than ever before.

The proliferation of national governments is not the only factor responsible for a multiplication of targets. Intelligence analysts now must cover international organizations and movements that had only a minor role in 1950 but that are major players today. Cartels such as OPEC can restrict the production and trade of natural resources such as petroleum. Religious movements can turn back the clock on modernizing societies. International terrorist movements threaten people and commerce throughout the world. Intelligence consumers demand in-depth coverage of these subjects, all of which were just marginal subjects for the intelligence community when it was created.

Similarly, the range of intelligence issues has grown. For most of its life, the Soviet/Eastern European division of ONE consisted of a political analyst, a military policy analyst, and an analyst who studied Soviet bloc relations. Most countries did not receive even this much attention. Today, just for the Soviet Union the U.S. intelligence community is required to cover the Soviet microelectronics industry, progress in nuclear and thermonuclear engineering, agriculture, the underground press, ethnic and religious relations within the Soviet state, space exploration and exploitation, Soviet economic and investment policies, theft and diversion of Western technology by Soviet intelligence services, and so on.

But the problem is not just in the collection of a greater volume of information to satisfy the demands of intelligence consumers. Processing and cataloguing this information so that it can be used by analysts and, eventually, intelligence consumers is itself a challenge. Just consider, for instance, the speed at which modern technical intelligence systems operate. Current intelligence collection systems can produce five or ten times as much data in the same amount of time as their counterparts of just ten years ago, which in turn produced information five to ten times as quickly as their predecessors ten years before that. This raw information can be invaluable, but only if the community can transform it into useful intelligence.

The Multiplication of Consumers

The growing demand intelligence consumers have for information would be difficult enough, but in addition to this there are also more intelligence consumers who are doing the demanding.

When the National Security Act of 1947 was adopted, creating the Central Intelligence Agency and the modern U.S. intelligence community, the number of officials the intelligence community had to support was relatively small. Today, in contrast, the White House staff alone has more than doubled in size during the past four decades. Harry Truman was supported by a White House staff of about 250 individuals; Ronald Reagan was supported by a White House staff of about 600. The State Department, the command structure of the military, and other organizations concerned with national security have also grown at respectable rates. In 1949, for example, the Army, Navy, and Air Force together accounted for 864 generals and admirals; by 1988 they accounted for 1,046 such officers. As the range of U.S. foreign commitments grew, so did the bureaucracy, and the demand for intelligence followed. These developments all reflect the increase in scope and complexity of U.S. foreign policy.

Furthermore, the intelligence community now is required to address economic and social questions that were previously minor concerns. The demand for economic information on countries such as the Soviet Union, for example, was a direct result of the Cold War, where conflict assumed the form of economic competition. George Kennan's doctrine of containment argued that if Soviet aggressiveness were checked for a sufficient period of time, eventually economic and social pressures would force the Soviets to address domestic demands, and this would force the Soviet leadership to adopt a more conciliatory international policy; thus, the welfare of the Soviet economy itself naturally became a matter of concern for U.S. policymakers. Similarly, as the Third World became a more pressing concern in U.S. policy, the need for data on commodity prices and likely decisions by OPEC emerged as an increasingly important requirement.[19]

And, in addition to the demand for more information and coverage of new targets, the intelligence community now also is presented with requirements for intelligence from organizations that previously did not need such support. Agencies such as the Drug Enforcement Administration and Coast Guard, which are assigned the mission of stopping the illegal shipment of drugs into the United States, have presented the community with their own specialized requirements, for example. Even Congress, which has taken a more active role on arms control and military planning, has certain intelligence requirements.

New Challenges for Collection

A third feature of the new intelligence environment is the difficulty of collecting intelligence and the complexity of turning raw data into useful information.

The intelligence community's most important target, of course, remains the Soviet Union, and the Soviets use a variety of "camouflage, concealment, and deception" measures (or "CC&D") to confound U.S. intelligence systems. These techniques range from the simple, such as throwing camouflaged tarpaulins over missiles, to the exotic, such as encrypting the telemetry from missile tests.[20] But the problem is compounded by the fact that targets that formerly were unaware of intelligence techniques have become more knowledgeable. Virtually any political, business, or military leader today knows how easily telephones can be tapped, and most of the basic techniques of SIGINT are an open secret. Even armies in many less-developed countries now take steps to conceal their facilities from airborne or spaceborne reconnaissance systems. During the Falklands War, for instance, Argentine forces built mock shell craters on the airstrip at Port Stanley in order to outwit U.S. satellite imagery, which the Argentineans assumed the United States was providing the British.

Add to this the modern technology totalitarian governments can use to enforce their rule—television surveillance, listening devices, electronic locking devices, computers for tracking dissidents, and so on—and one can appreciate the scope of the problem. The balance between offense and defense is always shifting in the technology of intelligence, but there can be little doubt that, overall, the struggle is taking place at a higher, more expensive level of competition. Some penetration and collection problems can be solved by better technology, but advanced technology presents its own problems for managing intelligence. The technological wizardry of intelligence collection can be incredibly expensive, meaning that the availability of such systems is limited, and this increasingly forces intelligence managers to make hard choices in selecting both which systems to build and the targets they will cover.

If anything, the challenge of collection will become greater in the future. The technology necessary for protecting information, such as encryption devices for communication systems, is becoming less expensive and is available on the open market. (Even HBO encrypts its satellite transmissions today in order to prevent nonpaying television viewers access to *Beverly Hills Cop*.) Usually the United States has a technological advantage and can often defeat such measures, but this is not always so, and, in any case, having to overcome such measures inevitably adds to the cost of intelligence.

As will be seen, the expense and complexity of current intelligence systems also introduces other difficulties. The growing cost of technical collection systems has made many of them what an economist would call "lumpy goods"—assets that can produce an enormous amount of intelligence but that also require a large initial investment before any intelligence can be collected at all. For example, often one cannot buy just a little SIGINT capability for a few thousand dollars. Rather, in order to collect any signals intelligence at all, one might have to buy an entire satellite system, and this is likely to cost several hundred million dollars. Unless the intelligence community antes up the entire cost, it will collect nothing, and, even after the system is introduced, it can be difficult to make small adjustments in collection capabilities. Additional capability often must be bought in increments of several million dollars. The rising cost of collection also increases the importance of planning, as building the wrong collection system can be a very, very expensive mistake.

Complex collection systems require long lead times for development, and to be affordable they must remain in operation for many years. The U-2 reconnaissance aircraft, for instance, can trace its origins to the early 1950s, when it was first proposed by Lockheed to the CIA. The aircraft first entered service in 1956, was eventually turned over to the Air Force for tactical missions, and will probably remain in service into the next century. During this fifty-year period, the U-2 will have been adapted for missions ranging from collecting imagery over the Soviet Union, to collecting electronic intelligence in Central Europe, to monitoring the "hole" in stratospheric ozone over Antarctica. The extended lifetimes of modern collection systems mean intelligence officials are required to anticipate intelligence requirements and plan the system's operation far into the future. In the case of signals intelligence, for example, intelligence planners have to anticipate what kinds of signals—the frequency, method of transmitting, possible encryption measures to be overcome, and so on—will produce the most lucrative intelligence sources in the year 2000 and beyond.

New Challenges for Analysis

Analyzing data is also much more complex today than it was thirty or forty years ago.

According to one story, Joseph Stalin was especially impatient with intelligence analysts. Once, it is said, an NKVD officer briefing Stalin began to explain the method he used to analyze his data. Stalin cut short the presentation, pounded his fist on the table, and shouted: "I don't want your theories—just give me the facts, give me the cables!" This story is probably apocryphal, but it does illustrate how complex intelligence analysis has become. If Stalin were alive today and said "Just give me the cables," he would likely be left holding an unreadable computer printout of binary code. As in the case of collection, analysis has become more complex. Consider just the task of developing an order of battle for Soviet strategic missiles, for example. To estimate the characteristics and deployments of Soviet missiles, U.S. intelligence analysts must use a variety of data, ranging from telemetry, imagery, reporting from emigrés and other human sources, records of Soviet tool purchases and material acquisitions on the world market, occasional samples of Soviet military hardware, and so on. None of the information is complete, and much is often faulty. Analysts then have to use these data to "reverse engineer" and deduce the characteristics of a missile that they have not seen and, most likely, will never see.

Even if the data were good, the models analysts use are complex and depend greatly on the assumptions one makes. For example, if an analyst changes his assumptions so that Soviet ICBMs are believed to be 30 percent less accurate and their warheads 5 percent less efficient—both relatively minor adjustments—the "single shot kill" probability estimated for a Soviet ICBM against an American Minuteman silo can fall from about eight out of ten to about three out of ten. The new estimate on Soviet ICBM accuracy could lead an analyst to change his interpretation of the missions the Soviets assign to their ICBM force. Rather than believing Soviet missiles are intended to destroy U.S. strategic weapons, the analyst might conclude that the missiles were aimed against U.S. cities—and this, in turn, would probably lead an analyst to a different interpretation of Soviet planning for nuclear war and the belief of Soviet leaders in whether nuclear war is "winnable."

Similar problems occur in political and economic analysis. In the early days of the intelligence community, political and economic analysis was relatively simple. At the time, facts about foreign countries were scarce, and intelligence analysts directed much of their efforts just toward developing this information. Indeed, for many years providing such basic information concerning geography, climate, urbanization, and so forth was a major function of national intelligence.*

Today the political and economic analysis used in the intelligence community is often much more complicated. To estimate the economic performance of other countries, the community has developed a number of specialized statistical and econometric models that are often as complex as those used for analyzing technical weapons systems. Such models have also been used to predict likely outcomes of elections and other political events.

This complexity of analysis produces ripple effects

---

* Much of this information was published in the *National Intelligence Surveys*—book-length summaries the intelligence community prepared for each country in the world. The U.S. intelligence community stopped publishing the *National Intelligence Surveys* in 1970, when it was clear that the information contained in the survey was readily available in the public sector. This evolution illustrates how the intelligence community is usually most appreciated when it concentrates on producing information that the public sector ignores because the information lacks a large audience or simply because the information is too expensive or too difficult to collect.

throughout the intelligence process. For instance, in the past when two analysts disagreed on an assessment, the dispute could usually be settled by deciding which analyst had the better data. Today disagreements often hinge on the assumptions and logic of complex models, so supervisors up the organizational ladder need to be able to understand these methods in order to settle the differences or develop new projects to develop the analysis necessary to settle the differences, and this, too, increases the demand for sophisticated analytic skills.

Planning analysis is largely a matter of planning people, and planning people for intelligence analysis can be as difficult as planning machines and organizations. The skills required by intelligence analysts today reflect the subjects the intelligence community covers, and, as we have seen, these encompass a broad range and can be highly specialized. So, whereas thirty years ago the intelligence community might have needed an analyst conversant in Russian terminology for rocket propellants, today the community needs this analyst, *and* another who has learned, say, the technical terminology of silicon chemistry in Japanese in order to assess developments in the world microprocessor industry, *and* another who knows the terminology of nuclear weapons in the dialects of Urdu prevalent in Pakistan in order to monitor nuclear proliferation. Presumably such people can be found or trained if one anticipates political, economic, and social trends correctly, yet it is becoming increasingly difficult to make such forecasts.

The New Politics of Intelligence

Another development affecting intelligence today is the changing American political scene. The politics of intelligence today is more open, the number of players who make intelligence policy has multiplied, and the values of the American public have shifted in several important dimensions. Each of these developments presents additional challenges for intelligence.

It is difficult to underestimate the change in attitudes toward secrecy during the past four decades. For example, when the National Security Act of 1947 was passed by Congress, there was virtually no debate on the provisions establishing the intelligence community; it was considered too sensitive.

Freedom of speech and freedom of the press are intrinsically desirable as civil rights, of course, but they are also essential to the operation of democracy. Ideas and information are the motors that move the democratic process. Restricting speech and the press restricts the ability of citizens to make democracy respond to their preferences. Without freedom of expression, citizens and elected representatives would be unable to explain and to reframe issues, and so would be unable to upset current policy and replace it with one of their own. Unfortunately, free-flowing information and public debate is usually the opposite of what is needed to protect intelligence sources and methods.

The past forty years have produced a series of court decisions and legislative initiatives that, for the most part, have made intelligence information more difficult to protect. The courts have ruled that the government can stop a person from disclosing classified information if the individual has accepted a secrecy agreement (as all intelligence community employees and contractors must do before acquiring access), and they have upheld penalties for violating these agreements, but they have usually ruled against most restrictions on nonemployees.

The most important test of the prerogative of the media to publish restricted information was the Pentagon Papers case, in which the Supreme Court affirmed the right of the *New York Times* to publish excerpts from a classified history of the Vietnam War prepared by the Department of Defense. The court ruled that, barring a "clear and present danger," restrictions on the media were unconstitutional. Since this broad affirmation of the media's prerogative, qualifications have been imposed on two fronts: penalties on the government officials presumably responsible for unauthorized disclosures and restrictions on the media that appear to meet the "clear and present danger" criterion—though the basic ruling has stood firm.*

The reluctance of the courts to limit the free flow of information has been reinforced by the reluctance of Congress to impose additional restrictions on classified information. With only a few exceptions, Congress has refused to impose criminal penalties on those who disclose classified information. Indeed, by passing the Freedom of Information Act (or FOIA, as it is better known), Congress significantly expanded access to intelligence information. Under the provisions of the FOIA, citizens and noncitizens alike can request all materials a government agency has on a particular subject. The FOIA exempts operational intelligence files and properly classified information, but the act has greatly expanded the amount of information available on the structure and operation of the intelligence community and on old operations deemed suitable for disclosure.

Information about intelligence activities will never be as readily available as some civil libertarians would like nor as restricted as some intelligence professionals might like, but the openness of the U.S. intelligence community is extraordinary among nations. Only a minority of countries have any effective laws protecting the freedom of the press, but even most of these countries allow their governments to restrict at least some information when it is deemed "in the national interest." The best example is Britain, whose Official Secrets

* For example, in 1972 the courts ruled that Victor Marchetti, a former CIA employee, had to submit the book he had written about the CIA to the agency for security review. In 1980 the courts upheld civil penalties against Frank Snepp, a CIA officer who violated this requirement. And, most recently, Samuel L. Morison, a naval intelligence analyst, was convicted in 1985 under criminal laws for passing satellite reconnaissance photographs to a British journal, *Jane's Defence Week*, even though the government had not proved actual damage had been done to U.S. intelligence by the publication of the photographs. However, these decisions have affected only those individuals who themselves have access to classified materials; the courts have been firm in maintaining the precedent of the Pentagon Papers case as it applies to the press and other nongovernment employees.

Act has been upheld and used by Conservative, Labour, and Liberal governments.[21] Yet the idea of an American Official Secrets Act has been repeatedly rejected by presidents of both parties, as well as by most members of Congress. In specific cases where a substantial danger to intelligence operations can be demonstrated, Congress has been willing to impose restrictions, but these have been rare. The most notable of these rare exceptions is the 1982 Intelligence Identities Act, which imposes criminal penalties for disclosing U.S. agents and intelligence officers operating under cover. At the time, publications such as *Counterspy* were openly dedicated to exposing U.S. intelligence operations wherever possible. Many legislators believed that this not only put U.S. intelligence officers in danger but it also made foreign intelligence services and potential agents reluctant to cooperate with the United States. The Identities Act meets the "clear and present danger" criterion, but it is most notable for being an exception to the general rule; the only other information whose publication Congress has made a crime under federal statute is certain information pertaining to the design of nuclear weapons protected under the Atomic Energy Act of 1956.

Taken together, the net effect of these trends is that (a) the government can deter disclosure with heavy penalties on individual employees, assuming they are identified, but (b) once the information is out, there is virtually no way that the government can restrict its dissemination, and (c) the right to information about intelligence has, within limits, been specifically affirmed and protected. As a result, U.S. intelligence policy is destined often to be made in an environment of public debate. It is unlikely that this trend is going to change, for the economic and political pressures for openness are too great, so the intelligence community will simply need to learn how to operate effectively in this environment.[22]

Another political development is the new role of Congress. Congressional oversight of intelligence has developed through three stages. In the first stage, roughly from the end of World War II to the early 1970s, Congress played a very limited role in U.S. intelligence policy. Secret subcommittees of the Armed Services and Appropriations Committees in the House of Representatives and Senate had total responsibility for congressional oversight. These subcommittees were small and had limited staffs, and so were unable to scrutinize intelligence policy closely. Even more important, though, the members of the intelligence subcommittees did not believe Congress should become deeply involved in intelligence matters.

The second phase of congressional oversight—from the early 1970s to the late 1970s—was at the other extreme and might charitably be called "oversight in depth." As part of the general reaction to the disclosures in the early 1970s of questionable or illegal conduct by the intelligence community, Congress passed the Hughes-Ryan Amendment in 1974, which effectively allowed almost any committee having jurisdiction over some aspect of intelligence to request intelligence officials to testify before it. At its peak, this resulted in over 250 members of Congress and much of their staff having access to intelligence information.

Legislators soon realized that this arrangement created impossible problems for security. So, in 1976 the Senate created a single oversight committee for intelligence. The House established a similar committee the following year. This began a new phase of congressional oversight, representing a compromise between ignoring oversight and endangering sources and methods.

Intelligence officials have had to adapt to these changes in oversight procedures. In the early years of the community and the first phase of oversight, intelligence officials did not concern themselves much with congressional affairs. In the second phase, the interest of the intelligence community was mainly in combating the hostility posed by the legislative branch. In the current phase, intelligence planners find themselves having to learn the policy and budgetary tactics familiar to most other federal officials, such as the Secretary of Defense or Secretary of Housing and Urban Development. For example, intelligence officials have had to master the art of legislative lobbying. The difference is that most intelligence officials have been raised in a culture that stresses secrecy and sharing information only with those having a clear "need to know." The relationship between Congress and the intelligence community has thus often been one of suspicion and has been strained significantly at least twice since the current oversight system was adopted: once, in 1984, over the mining of Nicaraguan harbors, and again, in 1986, with the disclosure of the Iranian arms initiative and the diversion of funds to the anti-Sandanista guerrillas.

The larger oversight role Congress demanded was really just part of a general trend of a legislature that was becoming more active on most national security issues: war powers, military reform, defense acquisition, arms control, and so on, in addition to intelligence. People may argue whether this legislative activism is a good fact or a bad fact, but it is nevertheless a fact. Congress has become a major player in national security policy. For intelligence planners, this means that Congress itself now has a larger stake in intelligence policy. For example, representatives with an interest in arms control have supported spending for the intelligence systems necessary for monitoring a treaty effectively. And, as one might have expected, intelligence officials have been more than willing to point out the contribution an intelligence system makes to arms control verification when they think it will improve its prospects for funding on the Hill. Congress has also become a major intelligence consumer, meaning that the concerns of Congress need to be reflected in national intelligence requirements.

New Roles and Expectations for Intelligence

One other new development is the role intelligence sometimes has in the American political process. More than ever before, intelligence is expected to settle what are often really political disagreements. More laws, congressional resolutions, and policy directives stipulate that certain actions will be carried out once certain conditions have been met and then leave it to the intelligence community to determine whether these conditions have indeed been met. This has dragged the intelligence community into what are not really questions about intelligence methods or the quality of data but questions of policy. Not only is intelligence poorly suited for settling such political questions; using intelligence in such contexts can endanger sources and methods and thus actually lead to the loss of the intelligence necessary for an informed consideration of the issues.

Arms control verification and Soviet violations of arms control treaties are probably the best example of this phenomenon. For example, in 1986 the United States had to decide whether to comply with strategic weapons limits imposed by SALT II. The agreement was beginning to constrain improvements the Reagan administration planned for U.S. forces. For the preceding three years, the intelligence community had reported a number of Soviet violations of SALT I and SALT II. These violations included the testing of more than one new ICBM, the testing of antiaircraft radar systems in conjunction with antiballistic missile tests, the construction of phased-array radar sites in prohibited areas, and others. The problem for U.S. officials was whether U.S. intelligence on these violations was solid enough to justify retaliation. Intelligence usually contains at least some ambiguity and will inevitably have difficulty in resolving such questions. Also, U.S. officials had to consider whether the intelligence they could make public would convince the American people that a strong U.S. response was warranted and whether whatever intelligence they did make public would compromise sources and methods.

In sum, the intelligence environment of today is considerably different from that which existed when the intelligence community was first founded, and the future success of the community will depend greatly on how well it deals with this new environment. Fortunately, unlike the founders of the modern U.S. intelligence community, U.S. leaders have almost forty years of experience on which to base their plans for improving strategic intelligence. As we shall also see, much of this experience has been made public, so it is possible for us to test ideas concerning the production of intelligence with a growing body of literature on the actual performance of the intelligence community.

TWO

Intelligence and Planning

Many people who work in intelligence describe the production of intelligence as a "cycle" or process consisting of these basic steps:

— determining the information intelligence consumers require;

— collecting the data needed to produce this intelligence; and

— analyzing the collected data and disseminating the resulting intelligence to consumers.

As one might expect, the intelligence cycle is one thing in principle and quite another in practice. Most bureaucracies rarely operate precisely according to flow charts, theoretical models, and organizational tables. Figure 2.1 shows roughly how this process works in practice and the close relationship that is required between intelligence producers and intelligence consumers. Still, the concept of an intelligence cycle is a good place to start in describing how the intelligence community operates, if only because this is how most people probably believe intelligence *should* be produced: it is logical, one step follows from another, and there is an efficient division of labor. Moreover, most intelligence failures can be classified as problems that arise when one or more steps in this process breaks down.

The Intelligence Cycle and Intelligence Failures

Before taking apart the process to see what makes it work (and not work), we need a better understanding of just what an "intelligence failure" really is. As we shall see, intelligence

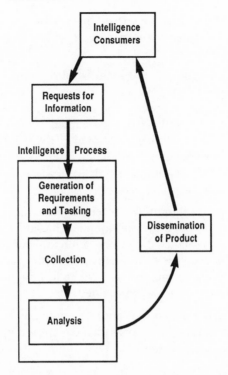

FIGURE 2.1

The Intelligence Consumer-Community Relationship

failures can take many forms. The most familiar kinds of failure are probably those that can be documented, such as a National Intelligence Estimate that proves to be incorrect. But there are other kinds of failures, some of which are more subtle. For instance, consider the following examples:

— The United States deploys a "smart munition" but lacks the data necessary to program the guidance system so that it can be used against all of the targets its developers intended.

— A White House official responsible for our policy in Southeast Asia regularly receives the *National Intelligence Daily* and the latest NIEs on the political situation in Vietnam but feels that these publications do not seem relevant to the problems with which he must deal every day.

— An advisor to the President is told to develop a plan to prevent U.S. arms dealers from circumventing the embargo on weapons to South Africa; he receives excellent intelligence from the United States and South Africa, but he thinks that some of the intermediaries may be meeting in Sweden and does not know how to get the information he needs from there.

— The United States adopts a stringent policy of interdicting illegal immigrants seeking to enter the United States; although officials identify the satellite and aircraft surveillance the Immigration and Naturalization Service requires to implement this program, no one takes the steps necessary to see that these intelligence resources are actually provided.

— The Army deploys an antihelicopter gun with insufficient range when it uses uncorroborated intelligence that underestimates the range of Soviet air-to-ground missiles.

— In his weekly intelligence briefing prepared for key State Department officials, an intelligence officer includes an item warning of a new terrorist alert in a Middle East country to which the officials are travelling, but the warning goes unheard because the officials found the hour-long briefings to be an inefficient use of their time and stopped attending.

As these examples illustrate, intelligence can fail not only when the contents of an estimate is simply wrong. Successful intelligence requires every part of the intelligence cycle to be carried out successfully. Missing any step can mean the failure of the intelligence product as a whole—a fact that suggests just how difficult managing the production of strategic intelligence can be.

Ascertaining Intelligence Needs

As Figure 2.1 shows, the first step in intelligence is to determine what intelligence consumers need to know and then to develop a coordinated plan that assigns organizations within the intelligence community responsibilities for producing this information. Usually these plans take the form of "requirements lists" that specify what data need to be collected and what analysis products need to be prepared. Collectors and analysts both prepare such plans, although, in common usage, the term "requirements" usually refers to collection; analysis organizations prepare "production plans" or "research programs." The process of turning these requirements or plans into instructions for specific action is called "tasking."

Collection requirements for the intelligence community as a whole are currently developed by the Director of Central Intelligence through his supporting secretariat, the Intelligence Community Staff (or, as it is usually called, the "IC Staff"). The IC Staff prepares target priority lists for both allocating the use of existing collection systems and for developing new systems. These lists are circulated within the intelligence community so that each agency in the community can incorporate these priorities into its own planning process.

Most agencies within the intelligence community have management staffs that prepare the agency's own requirements or programs. For example, the Director of the Defense Intelligence Agency is also the manager of the General Defense Intelligence Program (GDIP), which includes all "national" intelligence programs run by the Army, Navy, and Air Force (that is, those that have a governmentwide audience). The DIA Director prepares his plan for intelligence production annually, the Defense-Wide Intelligence Program (D-WIP), which in turn is used as guidance by the services in preparing their own programs.

Agencies responsible for analysis also develop plans that are at least nominally shaped by guidelines from above, but overall there is less coordination for analysis than for collection. One example of such a plan is the annual research program prepared by the CIA's Deputy Director for Intelligence, which assigns specific projects to each DDI office. Similarly, the Director of the DIA prepares the Defense Department's Delegated Intelligence Plan, which assigns pieces of the defense intelligence analysis pie to various agencies within the armed services. (When prepared for national consumers, Defense Department intelligence is usually issued under the DIA logo, even though it may have been prepared by, say, the Air Force Foreign Technologies Division.)

Collection

Once intelligence requirements are determined, the next step in the intelligence cycle is to collect the necessary data. Intelligence collection is traditionally divided into three disciplines: signals intelligence (SIGINT), human intelligence (HUMINT), and imagery intelligence (occasionally called "IMINT").

Collection responsibilities are distributed throughout the community. Most agencies have at least some responsibility for both collection and analysis. For example, the CIA includes both the Directorate of Operations, which collects clandestine HUMINT, and the Directorate of Intelligence, which produces analysis. The Air Force includes both wings that fly reconnaissance aircraft and analytic organizations responsible for developing assessment of foreign aircraft. The State Department publishes informational cables from embassies and produces analysis through the Bureau of Intelligence and Research (INR).

Strictly speaking, the two organizations with the largest responsibility for collection—the National Security Agency (NSA) and the agency responsible for operating reconnaissance satellites—are authorized only to collect and process intelligence data. Analysis of reconnaissance photography is carried out by the National Photographic Interpretation Center (NPIC) and various units in CIA and DIA, while "raw" signals intelligence is distributed among most analytic agencies on a need-to-know basis, where it is used in reports and estimates.

In practice, however, NSA also carries out what amounts to analysis, as it is often difficult to distinguish between the "processing" and "analysis" of signals intelligence. For example, translation is usually considered a part of SIGINT processing, but since it is impossible to translate all intercepts, signal intelligence translators have to choose which ones to process. This choice requires the translator to know which ones are important, and knowing which ones are important requires the translator to have a working knowledge of the subject matter. As a result, a translator at NSA may know as much—or more—about the target of the intercept as the analyst at CIA or DIA who uses the data, and, indeed, the process of selecting a signal to be intercepted is by nature a process of analysis.

Moreover, many SIGINT intercepts can stand on their own and really need little analysis. As a result, NSA has sometimes bypassed the analytic community and provided its SIGINT product directly to policymakers, a practice that has occasionally led to friction among top-level intelligence officials. It was, for example, sometimes a contentious issue between Stansfield Turner and Bobby Inman when the two admirals were, respectively, Director of Central Intelligence and Director of NSA. Other agencies responsible primarily for collection, such as the CIA's Directorate of Operations, have also been known for frequently engaging in such "end runs." This is especially true in the case of extraordinarily sensitive human sources, when most analysts are excluded from the distribution list because of the need for compartmentation and security.

One can sympathize with the intelligence collector. Almost any intelligence official prefers to have his agency's capabilities demonstrated directly to the President rather than buried in a coordinated research paper or analytical report. And, strictly speaking, the fastest way to get the product to the consumer is through bypassing the process of all-source analysis, interagency coordination and production. Still, when bypassing the analysts, a collector runs the risk of presenting the consumer a selective—and possibly inaccurate—picture of events, and certainly one that has not been corroborated by other forms of data.[1]

Analysis

Analytic units exist throughout the intelligence community. The largest and best-known include the CIA's Directorate for Intelligence; the DIA's Directorate of Research and Directorate of Estimates; and the State Department's Bureau of Intelligence and Research. However, there are many other smaller, less well-known units that contribute a substantial amount of the total output of the community.

Each of the armed services, for example, has its own science and technology analytic agencies: Foreign Technologies Division and Space Division for the Air Force, the Missile and Space Intelligence Center for the Army; and the Naval Intelligence Service Center for the Navy. Also, with one exception, each of the unified and specific commands has its own intelligence unit. (The exception is U.S. Central Command, which, despite its having responsibility for U.S. forces in the Middle East and Persian Gulf, must rely upon DIA in Washington for most of its intelligence support.)[2] And, in addition to all of these organizations, a considerable amount of technical intelligence is carried out by outside contractors, ranging from quasi-official agencies such as Los Alamos and Lawrence Livermore Nuclear Laboratories (responsible for many nuclear intelligence matters) to independent corporations, such as U.S. defense companies that provide cost assessments of foreign weapon systems.

The Intelligence Cycle in Practice

Ideally one might expect the history of a hypothetical assessment of the Soviet T-80 battle tank to be as follows: the Army plans to develop a new antitank missile and needs to know what capabilities the weapon needs in order to be able to destroy Soviet tanks. The IC Staff, learning of this, includes "information on Soviet armor systems" as an item in its annual listings of requirements. This requirement is passed to intelligence collectors and analysts so that they can incorporate it into their own plans. For instance, satellite operators might include Soviet tank factories or armor depots in their targeting plans, and analysts might include a report on the T-80 in their annual program for intelligence studies. The collectors then gather necessary raw data, and, finally, analysts use these data to develop a report that includes an estimate of the thickness of the T-80's armor and its resistance to various warheads. This report would then be delivered back to the Army, which would use it in drafting the specifications for its new antitank missile.

Unfortunately, the cycle does not always work as effectively in practice as it does in principle. One key reason is that intelligence planning in the U.S. intelligence community often resembles, ironic as it may seem, management practices in the Soviet Union: planning is highly centralized; planners are supposed to respond to the needs of consumers but are in fact insulated from them; and there is often little connection between satisfying the needs of an intelligence consumer and being rewarded for one's efforts.

If the intelligence community is sometimes as isolated from policymakers as Gosplan is from Soviet consumers, it is to be expected that some of the same problems result, too: just as Soviet consumers are frequently dissatisfied with the selection of merchandise and Soviet goods remain unsold on store shelves because they do not meet consumer expectations, intelligence consumers are often left dissatisfied with the intelligence product they receive, and a good amount of intelligence production in the United States appears to go unread. Intelligence planners approach their tasks with the best of intentions, but centralization is generally not the most effective way to respond to the needs of a diverse and growing audience. Sometimes intelligence requirements get lost in the bureaucratic shuffle; sometimes intelligence officials are unable to cut through the organizational red tape; and sometimes intelligence officials fail to respond because there is little incentive for them to do so.

Much of this difficulty in planning and managing U.S. intelligence is simply a result of having two objectives that usually cannot be achieved simultaneously: making the most effective use of a limited set of intelligence resources while at the same time responding to each intelligence consumer's requirements quickly and efficiently. The types of organization needed to achieve each objective are diametric opposites.

Because national intelligence resources are limited, someone has to determine how they will be allocated. Someone needs to determine whether, for instance, the Air Force's requirement for satellite imagery for analyzing Soviet aircraft should have priority over the Army's need for satellite imagery to detect a Warsaw Pact invasion of the Central Front in Europe, or vice versa. Making these kinds of allocations requires that the intelligence planners have the "big picture" of national intelligence needs and the authority to allocate resources, and this is why so much intelligence planning is centralized. Unfortunately, centralizing the management of intelligence this way can make the intelligence community less responsive in meeting the requirements of its consumers, since the best way to make intelligence responsive to the consumer is to put the tasking, collection, and analysis of intelligence under the consumer's direct control. Alas, there is not enough money to provide every intelligence consumer with its own dedicated intelligence community.

Of course, the formal procedures for producing intelligence provide only a partial picture of intelligence planning, and the informal processes that also take place can provide the necessary lubricant when the formal machinery sticks (just as the black market helps the Soviet economy survive). Individuals from the various intelligence organizations are constantly meeting with each other, and much of the groundwork for planning is laid out in this routine interchange. To some degree, the formal requirements are in part simply a codification of arrangements that have already been worked out. Also, a considerable amount of tasking (perhaps one-fifth in the case of many collection operations) is carried out on an ad hoc basis, so there is always bound to be some improvisation.

Even so, the formal process defines the objective the intelligence community tries to achieve, so when intelligence fails to meet the needs of its consumers, the requirements process is the logical place to begin to ask why.

THE PROBLEM OF PLANNING

The requirements process now managed by the IC Staff has evolved throughout the past four decades. To understand some of the problems that affect the requirements process today, one needs to understand how the process evolved.

The Requirements Process during World War II

Forty years ago, developing intelligence requirements was relatively simple in comparison to the procedures required today. The entire intelligence cycle for a particular type of intelligence was usually carried out by a single organization. For example, in Britain (from whence many of the organizational features of the U.S. intelligence community were inherited), airborne imagery during World War II was the responsibility of Photo Reconnaissance (PR) units attached to the Royal Air Force. These RAF units planned the missions, flew the aircraft, processed the film, analyzed the resulting imagery, and often even produced the finished intelligence reports. Everyone involved in the operation was RAF personnel, so planning was relatively straightforward.

The United States, which entered the war as ill-prepared for aerial reconnaissance as for most other intelligence functions, adopted the British model. Indeed, the first U.S. Navy reconnaissance analysts received their training at the British school at the Central Interpretation Unit at Dansfield House on the bank of the Thames.[3] The drawback of these procedures was that intelligence planning often reflected only the priorities of the particular service operating the collection system. Targets for other services were covered on an ad hoc basis. Though the particular organization operating the collection system received excellent service, other users often did not.

In fairness, it must be admitted that there were not many complaints with this arrangement. Agencies did not share data with each other, but then again requests for such data were the exception rather than the rule. "All-source" estimates were rare at the time. Analysts at the Office of Strategic Services, for example, were limited mainly to producing political assessments and thus could rely on OSS sources. Similarly, Army Air Force units that were responsible for damage assessments following bombing missions could rely mainly on aerial reconnaissance. This segmentation was reinforced by the compartmentation that always accompanies intelligence. Potential consumers were often unaware of the existence of data such as MAGIC, and so they simply never sought access.

These simple procedures were usually adequate, but when requirements did need to be coordinated across more than one agency, the limitations of the system became clear. At the beginning of the war, for example, Y Service (the RAF intelligence unit responsible for intercepting enemy signals) operated almost entirely in response to RAF intelligence requirements, such as locating German radar sites so that RAF mission planners could route bomber squadrons around them. As the war progressed, however, Y Service began to receive collection requests from other agencies as well. After cryptologists at Bletchley Park were able to decipher German Enigma traffic regularly, Y Service was assigned the additional mission of recording coded German radio communications traffic for the Secret Intelligence Service (SIS, also known as "MI-6"). Later, Y Service was also requested to collect radar signals for analysis by scientific intelligence units in the RAF and SIS. And, on top of all of this, by the end of the war, Y Service was expected to provide tactical SIGINT for military units at the front.

The coordination of all these requests was assigned to a Deputy Director of Intelligence in the Air Ministry, who was supposed to follow guidance from the military Chiefs of Staff and SIS. Alas, this guidance was often incomplete or contradictory, and so Y Service personnel in the field sometimes had to decide for themselves what they should cover. The result was what one might expect when one organization tries to meet the needs of another organization that is separated by three layers of coordination. Targets were often missed, requirements were left unfulfilled, and limitations on dissemination inevitably meant that some consumers were blindsided.[4]

Intelligence that required data collected by two or more different systems also presented problems. One illustration of the difficulties that could arise occurred when the Allied intelligence services tried to analyze German radar systems. Analyzing a radar system required imagery; analysts could estimate the characteristics and capabilities of a radar unit by the size and shape of its antenna. Unfortunately, radar sites were usually too small to locate on aerial photography without some tipoff of their general location. The solution was to fly photoreconnaissance aircraft periodically over France to "tickle" German air defense radar. When the Germans activated their radar to track the aircraft, Y Service traced the source of the signal, and Photo Reconnaissance Unit analysts would use this SIGINT to find the radar site in imagery, often taken by the same aircraft responsible for making the Germans activate their radar.[5] There was, however, no regular system for coordinating such combined operations; it was usually done on a case-by-case basis. The personal connections of intelligence officials and their working knowledge of who was whom in the British intelligence establishment were often the only way to ensure that requirements were met.

Sometimes the system worked; sometimes it did not. In the case of the assessment of the German missile program, for instance, Military Intelligence (the British Army's equivalent of the U.S. Army's G-2) inadvertently hamstringed the efforts of the rest of the British intelligence community to analyze the missile that later became known as the V-2. When Military Intelligence first received reports of the new missile, it asked Duncan Sandys, a member of the War Cabinet, to supervise a special assessment. In the process of organizing collection support for the project, Sandys instructed PR units to withhold imagery of Peenemunde from all other analysts. Unfortunately, these "other analysts" included R. V. Jones, head of scientific intelligence for the RAF and the SIS, who was also investigating the V-2 problem. Fortunately Jones was able to bypass this restriction by asking his SIS associates for reportage on Peenemunde from British agents and by obtaining "bootleg" imagery through his personal connections with officers in PR. The British were fortunate that Jones was able to circumvent compartmentation in this case, as his report was later a key factor in the decision to bomb Peenemunde, thus delaying the V-2 program.[6]

Postwar Intelligence Planning

After the war, the United States gradually centralized the planning of intelligence collection and analysis under the authority of the DCI. One reason for this was that the intelligence community began to carry out more "all-source reporting"—intelligence that combined SIGINT, imagery, and so forth—in estimates. Like the reorganization of the intelligence community, the trend toward all-source reporting was another response to the Pearl Harbor failure. American officials believed that a more comprehensive review of the available data would have revealed Japanese plans to attack the United States.

A second reason why planning became centralized was the rising cost of collection and the growing reliance on national intelligence collection systems, or systems intended to serve users throughout the intelligence community. Part of the cost resulted from the specialization of new collection systems. During World War II, a bomber could be modified to perform most photoreconnaissance missions, but by the 1950s specially designed aircraft such as the U-2 and, later, the SR-71 were required to penetrate the defenses of many opponents. These specialized systems were expensive, and as the cost of collection rose, each agency had to share collection systems.

This in turn required agencies to coordinate their collection requirements.

This trend toward centralization, however, has not occurred as quickly as the history of the legislation governing the intelligence community might suggest. Though the public has probably always thought of the Director of Central Intelligence as the country's "Master Spy" or "Chief Spook," the real leverage the DCI has been able to exercise over the intelligence planning and operations has lagged behind the control he was authorized by statute.

Most of the agencies within the intelligence community are organizationally part of the Department of Defense (in addition to some small-budget programs in the departments of State, Justice, the Treasury, and Energy). This is because, even though the DCI was designated as the official responsible for intelligence planning by the National Security Act of 1947, the act did not remove the agencies that were responsible for producing intelligence from the organizational structure and chain of command of their parent departments. So, organizations such as NSA, the Office of Naval Intelligence, and the Army's G-2 remained Department of Defense agencies.

As a result, even though the DCI could recommend guidelines for the budgets and day-to-day management of these organizations, real control over planning, personnel decisions, and operations remained with the parent departments. Even strong DCIs such as Allen Dulles, John McCone, and Richard Helms lacked control over the pursestrings and operations of most of the intelligence community outside that of the CIA.

Consider the development of intelligence community's budget, for example. In 1971, James Schlesinger, then an Assistant Director in the Office of Management and Budget, recommended that the DCI be given greater fiscal control. Richard Nixon approved this recommendation in a formal executive order. In response to the executive order, Helms, who was DCI at the time, prepared the first consolidated budget for the intelligence community, establishing the IC Staff in its current form in the process. Yet, as in the case of the National Security Act, the mere existence of the consolidated budget did not mean that the DCI really had his hands on the pursestrings. The budget prepared by the IC Staff under Helms really consisted of the CIA budget, plus whatever the Defense Department had approved for its various intelligence operations, plus relatively small amounts from the State Department for INR, Justice Department for FBI counterintelligence, and the Treasury Department and Atomic Energy Commission for their intelligence shops. Most budget decisions were still being determined by the Pentagon, and Helms had, according to William Colby, an "exquisite . . . sense of political realities" and knew that he lacked the backing if he tried to tell the Defense Department how much money to spend on its intelligence programs and how to spend it.[7]

Indeed, earlier attempts had been made to consolidate intelligence operations under the DCI, but they had also failed. The evolution of the Intelligence Community Staff—the DCI's primary management tool—had reflected a series of lost battles between the Director of Central Intelligence and the Secretary of Defense. The IC Staff had been created out of the existing Intelligence Resources Advisory Committee, which had in turn been created in 1971 out of the National Intelligence Resources Board, which had been established in 1968.[8] Each time, a formal order or directive had been issued to improve the DCI's leverage over intelligence spending but was rendered meaningless as Defense Department officials resisted.

The turning point in this bureaucratic struggle appears to have been the term of Stansfield Turner as DCI. Even though Turner himself failed to gain management control over the community, he set in place the procedures that would later be adopted by his successor, William Casey.

Turner had been given assurances by President-elect Carter that he would have the authority necessary to manage national intelligence.[9] Turner went ahead and established the procedures and organizations within the IC Staff to carry out this mandate. Under Turner, the IC Staff prepared the National Foreign Intelligence Program (NFIP), the first consolidated intelligence community budget submitted for review by Congress. Turner was assisted in his initiative by the fact that Congress had recently created the House Permanent Select Committee on Intelligence and the Senate Select Committee on Intelligence. The intelligence committees had been given responsibility for authorizing the intelligence community budget and needed the NFIP to serve as the basis for their authorization bills, and so they supported Turner in establishing the NFIP. Turner also created a separate National Intelligence Tasking Center, or NITC, which was to oversee the day-to-day operation of collection systems.

Although Turner created the management structure for centralizing intelligence planning, he, like previous DCIs, was himself unable to exercise much effective control. The Defense Department continued to resist giving up control over national intelligence programs contained in its budget, and, in the end, President Carter failed to provide Turner the support he required. The same was true of managing the operations of national collection systems. Although Turner probably won more individual battles than his predecessors, the agencies responsible for collection were able to circumvent most of the DCI's efforts to gain routine control by using a variety of strategies and tactics. For example, NSA, DIA, and other agencies responsible for intelligence collection were never put into a formal chain of command under the NITC. Combined with the fact that the head of the NITC held the civilian equivalent of a three-star flag rank, and the heads of NSA and DIA are themselves generally three-star admirals or generals, the NITC was unable to issue binding orders.

The organizations and procedures that Turner established, however, survived (with a few exceptions, such as the NITC). Casey, who succeeded Turner, had the backing of the President and the mandate of Executive Order 12333 which was approved in 1981 and which explicitly affirmed the DCI's authority over the peacetime operations of the Intelligence Community. Casey also had the advantage of growing defense and intelligence budgets, meaning he was required to plan growth rather than allocate cuts—which inherently creates less resistance. Casey thus succeeded where Turner did not and became the first Director of Central Intelligence who can be said to have had effective control over the resources of the national intelligence community.*

The DCI can now set the general direction of the national intelligence program, but even today he must operate under certain constraints. For example, the NFIP is a separate program from national defense, but the NFIP budget is still hidden inside the defense budget for reasons of security. As will be seen later, this creates indirect linkages between defense planning and intelligence planning (e.g., cutting defense spending can create pressure to reduce intelligence spending). Also, there are hidden strings that can tie the DCI's hands. For instance, although an Air Force officer managing a DIA intelligence collection program must follow the DCI's guidelines in developing his or her own annual collection plan, the program manager also realizes that he will eventually rotate back into the "real" Air Force. Knowing that the Air Force, not the DCI, will determine the success of his future career can and does affect the decisions of such a program manager when the priorities of the intelligence community and the Air Force collide (the same can also apply to foreign service officers on rotation to INR, Army officers rotating through NSA, and so on).

Planning Mechanisms

In the earliest years of the intelligence community, the DCI outlined his collection priorities in a master listing issued as a

* There is an ironic aspect to this story. One of Stansfield Turner's main opponents in establishing control by the DCI over intelligence planning was Bobby Inman, who was NSA Director during Turner's term as DCI. Like most previous NSA directors, Inman worked hard to protect NSA's autonomy. In 1981, however, Inman was appointed to the position of Deputy Director of Central Intelligence, where he was at least as important as Casey in developing community-wide, comprehensive plans for investment in intelligence systems and in establishing the role of the DCI as the chief authority over national intelligence planning.

National Security Council Intelligence Directive (NSCID). Gradually expanded over the years, this document listed individual intelligence targets and assigned them one of three levels of priority (later expanded to four levels). The current counterpart of this listing is Director of Central Intelligence Directive 1/2 (DCID 1/2, read as "D-skid-one-slant-two").[10]

Master lists such as DCID 1/2 itemize what a collection system should be pointing at or listening to and are useful in the day-to-day operation of collection systems. But such target lists have their limitations, as they do not describe the substance of what officials want to know. For example, a Deputy Assistant Secretary of State for Soviet and European Affairs would not say that she wants broad-area, false-color imagery of Ukrainian wheatfields at biweekly intervals; more likely, the official would say she wants to know whether the Soviets are going to have a grain shortage this year and what such a shortage would do to the Soviet economy. Planning systems such as DCID 1/2 do not respond to this kind of request well, so, even if the process works as intended, the intelligence product might not address the substantive questions of intelligence consumers.

William Colby appreciated this problem, and in response he added a new set of procedures for establishing intelligence requirements oriented around the substantive questions that intelligence consumers want answered. Colby called the document that emerged from this process the Key Intelligence Questions (KIQs). The first set of KIQs was published in 1973. By 1975 the KIQs included sixty-nine separate questions, about one-third of which dealt with the Soviet Union. Turner continued Colby's initiative by establishing the system that has continued to the present, the National Intelligence Topics (NITs). The NITs are essentially a refinement of the KIQs, originally consisting of ninety-nine topics determined to be the highest intelligence priorities of U.S. intelligence consumers.[11]

Yet the NITs also have a shortcoming. Although they identify the substantive questions intelligence consumers want answered, the NITs do not link the allocation of resources to intelligence priorities. These guidelines (like DCID 1/2) are developed separately from the budgets of the intelligence agencies. In other words, the guidelines are not firmly connected to real dollars. Program managers, who actually build the budgets for the collection systems and analytic agencies, are required only to indicate that their program addresses some item in the guidelines. There is almost always a high-priority item in the lists that can be used to justify a program. (Almost any space-based collection system, for example, can be used to collect at least some information from the Soviet Union.) Thus, DCID 1/2 and the NITs do not keep the program managers under a tight reign. Moreover, annual planning mechanisms such as DCID 1/2 and the NITs have a time horizon that is far too short for effective planning. A process that only establishes priorities for the coming year is not adequate for planning programs that require five or ten years to design, develop, and implement.

To tie budgeting more closely to the substantive questions of intelligence consumers and to extend the time horizon of the program manager, intelligence officials in recent years have periodically developed comprehensive, long-range planning systems and linked them directly to specific intelligence programs. For instance, in 1981 then-Deputy Director of Central Intelligence Bobby Inman supervised the development of the Intelligence Capabilities Plan. This plan drew together the types of questions the intelligence community would be expected to answer in the remainder of the decade, the difficulties the community would face in addressing these requirements, and the resources expected to be available.

So, to use a hypothetical example, where a NIT might say, "the third highest priority mission of the U.S. intelligence community is to warn the United States of a Warsaw Pact attack in Central Europe," the Intelligence Capabilities Plan would go on to say "and we are going to carry out this mission with improvements in air-breathing reconnaissance systems, new SIGINT assets, and, if necessary, elves in the Black Forest." Establishing this baseline, the plan then constructed a multi-year plan for addressing these requirements, providing guidelines to individual agencies for specific programs to be submitted to the DCI for inclusion in the National Foreign Intelligence Program.[12]

In a similar vein, in response to a request initiated by the Senate Intelligence Committee, in 1986 the Director of Central Intelligence developed a National Intelligence Strategy. The National Intelligence Strategy took long-range planning one step further by identifying specific missions that would be required of the intelligence community, such as monitoring arms control, maintaining a data base on Soviet military forces, etc. It then explained how the intelligence community intended to carry out these missions. The DCI's use of the NIS in his planning was reinforced when the congressional oversight committees used the National Intelligence Strategy in their own review of the intelligence community budget.

Planning Organizations for Collection

Collection tasking and planning the development of new collection systems is carried out by interagency committees sponsored by the IC Staff. These committees include representatives from agencies within the community and from intelligence consumers (although, as we shall see shortly, the membership of the committees is weighted in favor of representatives of the agencies responsible for operating the systems). Currently there are three publicly identified interagency committees that translate the DCI's requirements into specific tasking orders and plans for the development of new systems. These are the Committee on Imagery Requirements and Exploitation (COMIREX) for decisions affecting imaging systems, the SIGINT Committee for decisions on signals collection systems, and the HUMINT Committee for decisions affecting collection assets such as case officers, attachés, and embassies.[13]

The evolution of the IC Staff's system of interagency committees has in part reflected progress in technology and growth in the intelligence community and in part bureaucratic politics within the community. The SIGINT Committee, for example, traces its origins to the late 1940s and the U.S. Communications Intelligence Board (USCIB), a committee responsible for coordinating military communications intelligence systems on behalf of the Joint Chiefs. The Secretary of Defense briefly disbanded USCIB in favor of his own committee in 1949, but the board was reestablished in 1952 when the National Security Agency was founded.

The establishment of NSA created the need for a new planning system by precipitating one of the first chain of command problems in the postwar intelligence community. The National Security Agency was a national intelligence organization and thus was supposed to be under the control of the DCI. However, the agency was staffed mainly by military personnel, who were supposed to be under the control of the Secretary of Defense. USCIB was re-created to provide the DCI a vehicle for issuing general guidance for NSA operations, while leaving the Secretary of Defense responsible for the day-to-day operations of the agency. USCIB was renamed as the COMINT Committee in 1958 and was again renamed in 1962 as the SIGINT Committee when it was given responsibility for electronic intelligence (ELINT). The SIGINT Committee was later put into the IC Staff structure.[14]

A similar path of development was followed by COMIREX. The earliest national imagery coordination committee appears to have been the Ad-Hoc Requirements Committee, established in 1955 to support the CIA's U-2 program (although the Air Force already had its own units within the Air Staff to plan the use of its imagery collection aircraft). The introduction of satellite imagery transformed the Ad-Hoc Requirements Committee into the Committee on Overhead Reconnaissance by 1960. This committee was, in turn, reorganized as COMIREX in 1967, when its authority was extended to include Defense Department imagery systems and to coordinate the processing of the imagery, which would, for the most part, henceforth be undertaken by the newly created National Photographic Interpretation Center (NPIC), a joint CIA-DOD organization.[15]

The HUMINT Committee is a more recent development.

Though it can be assumed to follow the general pattern of the other two committees, few specific details concerning its operations have been released.

Each of the committees contains one subcommittee responsible for tasking and another subcommittee responsible for planning future systems. Tasking is usually straightforward, as it is relatively simple to translate DCID 1/2 into a set of specific instructions for the system operators. For technical systems, tasking is usually a matter of writing or modifying the computer program that directs the system. For human collection, tasking is a process of writing a list of categories of information to be gathered, which are then used to develop the collection plans for embassies and stations abroad and other HUMINT facilities.

Using DCID 1/2 and the NITs to plan future systems, on the other hand, is more complicated. Committee members must be able to anticipate both future collection requirements and the technologies that will be available. They also have to choose among the targets the proposed system will be capable of covering—and, in doing so, accept limitations in U.S. collection capabilities, many of which will persist for many years once the choice is made. For instance, the orbit necessary for a reconnaissance satellite to collect one kind of intelligence may preclude the collection of another kind of intelligence. The "lost" intelligence may have to await the development and funding of the next generation of satellites.

Ideally, these decisions should be made so that they respond to the needs of intelligence consumers. Yet, for a variety of reasons, this has not always been the case. For instance, most officials responsible for planning future collection systems have historically been the operators of the systems. Unfortunately, the operators are often the individuals in the intelligence cycle who have the least contact with the final users of intelligence. One reason operators play such an important role in designing new systems is that the people who operate the systems are usually the ones most familiar with the collection technology just over the horizon (so to speak). For example, James Killian, Edwin Land, and other presidential scientific advisors who had been instrumental in initiating the U-2 program were also influential in the decision to develop reconnaissance satellites.[16] Similarly, Richard Bissell, who supervised the U-2, went on to oversee some of the early intelligence satellite programs.[17]

A second reason operators are so influential in the design of collection systems is that they spend most of their time thinking about and working on the collection problem. As a result, they are often the first to discover a new approach that might have an intelligence payoff. One illustration of this occurred during World War II. In addition to collecting intelligence, SIGINT operators are responsible for "frequency search," the process of systematically sampling bands along the broadcast spectrum to detect transmissions that might have intelligence value. The equipment used for frequency search is usually the same used to collect intelligence, so SIGINT operators such as Y Service were often the first proponents of a new, specialized SIGINT system to collect a new set of signals for exploitation because they were the ones spinning the dials searching for frequencies on which the Germans were transmitting.[18]

A third reason operators have such influence in planning new systems is security. Information concerning the design and operation of collection systems is usually classified separately from the information actually produced by the system.* For example, during World War II ULTRA intelligence

---

* Currently such information is compartmented by "codewords"; these are additional restrictions placed on sensitive information after it is classified "secret" or "top secret," depending on its sensitivity.

For example, in the case of SIGINT, the information produced by a collection system might be classified as "Bob," the design and operation of the system might be classified as "John," and the processing of the information might be classified as "Bill" (actual codewords are themselves classified, as they could provide clues pointing to the existence of a particular category of information).

Access to information classified under a given codeword is granted on a "need to know" basis. Most analysts usually have little "need to know" the technical details of a system, so most would receive only Bob information; the designers and most operators of the system need to know both how the

was often disguised as being from some other source, such as human agents, so consumers often were unaware that they were even using SIGINT, let alone the nature of the technology that made it possible. Those who did recognize that their information was signals intelligence often did not know that the key ingredient that made the intercepts possible was the Allies' ability to break German ciphers.[19]

The result of this necessary compartmentation is that most of the people with a working knowledge of collection technology are the ones operating collection systems. They are also often among the few people who have access and are familiar with the entire operation of collection, tasking, and analysis. Relatively few analysts have such access, and those who do are usually in a managerial position rather than at the working level. So line analysts—who are frequently more attuned to the needs of the intelligence consumer than are the operators of a collection system—are often unable to contribute to the tasking or design of a collection system. Naturally, consumers, who are separated from collection by an additional layer of security, are in an even less advantageous position.

But compartmentation not only cuts analysts out of the planning process; it can also have a detrimental effect on the quality of whatever analysis is produced. Compartmentation requires that the origins of information be obscured. This affects an analyst's judgment of the quality or reliability of the data and, later, the consumer's judgment of the intelligence product. For example, because human sources are so vulnerable, when information from these sources is provided to analysts, the origin of the information is described in only general terms, e.g., "a source with access who has reported reliably in the past" (though exceptions are made to this rule on a limited basis). And, as the ULTRA case above illustrates, sometimes even the general category of a collection source

system works and how well it is performing, so they would usually be given access to both Bob and John. Some operators and most managers of the program would need to know how the entire system works and would thus have access to Bob, John, and Bill.

may be obscured, as when a SIGINT source is described in a way that makes it look like a HUMINT source, or vice versa.

As a result, analysts tend to discount these sources in favor of sources they know more about, even though this information may be less complete or less accurate. One illustration of this appears to have occurred in the failure of the U.S. intelligence community to predict the rapid escalation in petroleum prices during the early 1970s. U.S. analysts were familiar with the sources reporting from embassies in the Middle East, and these sources suggested that a significant market fluctuation was unlikely. By placing too much credence in these sources, the analysts disregarded other evidence that suggested that a price increase was indeed likely.[20]

Ironically, compartmentation is often strictest for what could be the most productive collection programs. This may occur, for example, when the intelligence collected is extraordinarily valuable but easily defeated if the operation is disclosed (examples include the 1955/1956 Berlin tunnel operation, where the CIA tapped landlines used by the Soviet military; once the operation was discovered, the Soviets immediately turned to alternative communication channels).[21] Compartmentation is also strict when disclosure of an operation would strain U.S. relations with other countries, as in the case of such operations as the CIA's U-2 program or Iranian SIGINT sites, which required the cooperation of countries bordering the Soviet Union, or politically delicate operations such as the salvage of a sunken Soviet submarine by the *Glomar Explorer*.[22] Such sensitive collection operations are usually planned and developed separately from other programs, and access to these programs is even more restricted than usual. This, of course, makes it even more difficult to achieve a working connection between planning, requirements, and consumer needs.

Yet, lest effective collection seem simply a matter of allowing analysts and consumers closer to the collection planning process, it also needs to be pointed out that rigidly linking collection requirements to consumers' demands for intelligence carries its own risks. One such risk is that it tends to reduce the opportunity for "entrepreneurship" by collection specialists. Often the value of a source of information cannot be determined until the information exists, is made available to the intelligence community, and someone finds a useful way to exploit it. Often data are used quite differently from how the collectors originally expected.

In other words, it is necessary to allow the community some "venture capital" for innovations in collection. Overly rigid, centralized intelligence planning has some of the same shortcomings as does centralized economic planning: it may seem like a rational way to distribute resources in an optimal fashion, but over the long run it stifles the creativity an intelligence organization requires. Unfortunately, today (as will be seen) the intelligence budget is stretched to the limit simply to cover those requirements that are based on specific consumer needs. Under these conditions it is difficult to justify "extra" funding with no immediately identifiable benefit. Thus, some device is needed to ensure the long-term health of the intelligence community by protecting the resources for covering "firm" targets while also providing some amount of additional resources for the "venture capital" the community needs to remain capable in the future.

Planning Intelligence Analysis

Ensuring that analysis responds to the needs of consumers presents a somewhat different set of problems. Even more so than collection, most analysis is planned and managed by individual agencies rather than at a communitywide level. So, for example, CIA analysis of politics, economics, and military affairs is planned by the Deputy Director for Intelligence; DIA analysis is planned by the Director of DIA; INR analysis is planned by the Assistant Secretary of State for INR; and so on. The main exceptions are NIEs and Interagency Intelligence Memoranda (IIMs), which are planned by the DCI with the support of the National Intelligence Council (NIC).

In most agencies, the head of the agency and his staff develop an annual production schedule for the year. These production schedules outline the major studies that are planned. The items included in any agency's production schedule come from a number of sources: National Intelligence Topics, staff recommendations, discussions with individuals throughout the national security community, and the judgment of the agency heads themselves. Usually the plans are updated quarterly, so most agencies are effectively on an annual planning cycle with adjustments being made every three months. The agencies publish their production plans and circulate drafts among intelligence consumers, so that, at least in theory, the consumers can comment on them.[23]

This rather regimented approach to planning intelligence production has been used from the earliest days of the modern intelligence community—indeed, from the days of the oss in World War II. William Langer, head of the oss's Research and Analysis Division, needed a system to organize and coordinate the reports that were being prepared by different analysts, especially when several analysts were working together on a single product. The situation was an unfamiliar one for Langer and his analysts, who had been brought up in academia. Political scientists and historians tend to work alone rather than in teams. Also, academicians usually do not have to meet firm deadlines for their research. To manage the problem, Langer required his analysts to submit schedules for completing their contribution to R&A's studies. By 1943, the R&A production plan looked essentially the same as those used in the intelligence community today: each manager listed the studies his office would prepare, the analyst leading the team responsible for each study, the resources that would be needed, the expected time of completion, and the probable customers.[24]

Just as current production plans can trace their origins to oss procedures, present-day intelligence publications such as DDI Intelligence Assessments and INR Intelligence Briefs can trace their ancestry to the R&A division reports produced at oss. These reports were essentially adaptations of the academic journal article—a medium familiar to oss analysts, who were, of course, drawn largely from academia. Indeed, the intelligence periodical also seems to have been around as long as the analysis production plan. As we have seen, the CIA established itself as an analytical agency by providing daily intelligence summaries for President Truman. But even during World War II, the Joint Chiefs published the *MAGIC Summary*, outlining the significant COMINT items collected during the preceding twenty-four hours. (This periodical was later supplemented with specialized army and navy editions, at which point the original publication was renamed the *Diplomatic Summary*.) The *MAGIC Summary* was an early ancestor of the SIGINT periodicals NSA produces today, just as the specially tailored *MAGIC Summary* provided to President Roosevelt as of 1944 can be considered a predecessor of the *President's Daily Brief* (PDB).

The actual products listed in the production plan can take various forms. Most, however, are "finished" intelligence publications—printed and bound intelligence memoranda and assessments, sometimes called "FININTEL." Although regularly published intelligence periodicals are usually not included as part of the production plan, the plan is developed with the assumption that the analysts working on the items included in the plan will also support publications such as the CIA's *President's Daily Brief* and *National Intelligence Daily*, the DIA's *Defense Intelligence Summary*, and INR's *Morning Summary*. The topics of the publications and those of the periodicals usually complement each other, so that an analyst working on an assessment of the future of beef production in Botswana is likely to produce a current article for the *National Intelligence Daily* if the price of cattle rises or falls substantially or unexpectedly.

QUALITY CONTROL AND CONSUMER RELATIONS

In a well-designed organization, quality control systems are built in. Intelligence analysts and managers should have a natural incentive to find out exactly what their consumers need to know and automatically adjust the intelligence product as necessary. But does the current system of planning and producing intelligence, as it has evolved, respond to the intelligence consumer? As one leading intelligence official has said, "Unless we are responding to what our consumers want and need to know, then essentially we in the intelligence community are doing nothing more than spending a lot of money to build a very expensive library."

One problem in ensuring quality control is that it is often quite difficult to assess whether a consumer's intelligence needs are being met. The quality of intelligence in routine, peacetime operations can be hard to measure from the consumer's perspective because the situations in which intelligence can prove pivotal, which would indicate if something were not working, are rather rare. Critical tests of intelligence, such as international economic crises or military interventions, do not occur often enough to assess the performance of analysts or their managers. Even "routine" events such as the deployment of a new type of Soviet ICBM may only occur every five or ten years.

The Director of Central Intelligence has had some type of quality control unit since 1972, when the Product Review Division was established. More recently the DCI has depended on a Senior Review Panel consisting of experienced analysts and a Product Evaluation Staff to review the quality of the intelligence product, but its effectiveness has been mixed. Although intelligence officials acknowledge the need for quality control, many of the officials who have taken part in the current review process have criticized these bodies for their inability to take corrective actions after identifying a problem; they are wholly dependent on the willingness of the DCI to make changes and then follow through to make sure that they are carried out. Moreover, these evaluation bodies are too small to monitor all intelligence products. This is why DCIs have used them sparingly—usually as a tangible response when faulty intelligence causes a costly foreign policy setback.

In any case, relying on special monitoring units is probably an inefficient way to make intelligence respond to the needs of consumers, and may even be counterproductive. Such bodies can alienate personnel within the intelligence community and disrupt operations when they are used. Unleashing the monitors becomes a signal that something has gone wrong, and that someone is going to have to pay. This, in turn, can naturally lead to resistance to making the use of such an office a routine part of the intelligence process.

Quality review panels probably serve their function most effectively simply by making clear when an intelligence failure has occurred. There is a natural reluctance on the part of intelligence officials to delegate their authority to a review board; this may explain why such boards have traditionally lacked the clout to take corrective actions and why such panels will inevitably depend on other officials. However, if an intelligence failure is demonstrated convincingly and the evidence circulated, it is usually difficult for intelligence officials to avoid taking some action in response. This is one reason why, overall, there has been a trend toward greater accountability in intelligence production. For example, the CIA maintains files for all analysts in the Directorate for Intelligence; each time an analyst prepares a product, it is put into his or her file. This file is used in promotion decisions so that, although it is not the only factor used in evaluating an analyst, it can at least be considered.

Another difficulty in making intelligence more responsive to the needs of consumers is that many of the best approaches pose risks to other goals, such as objectivity. For example, the intelligence community's responsiveness to consumers could be improved by putting the analyst closer to the normal chain of command in the national security bureaucracy. Of all the agencies in the national security community, currently the State Department probably goes furthest in combining policy authority with intelligence responsibilities. Foreign Service officers are expected to be collectors of information as well as implementors of policy. This also happens to be the practice in most private corporations.[25] For example, a multinational bank typically has an officer in the approval chain for a loan rescheduling who is expected to be familiar with the country in question. The officer's "intelligence estimate" consists of his approval or disapproval of the loan and is usually part of any explanatory memoranda transmitted with the decision.* Putting the intelligence analyst in the chain of command is bound to improve the responsiveness of intelligence. Most intelligence analysts have at least some incentive to be responsive to policy needs, and they usually will be responsive if they have the opportunity and are made aware of when an intelligence assessment is needed.

Alternatively, rather than inserting intelligence analysts into the line of command, one could simply improve the degree to which intelligence analysts are able to deal directly with their consumers. When tried in the past, this has usually improved intelligence. For example, during World War II, the British hardly used publications at all in distributing ULTRA intelligence. Instead, SIGINT was supplied to operational commanders in the field by Special Liaison Units (SLUs) assigned from Bletchley Park. The SLUs, which were given minimally processed intelligence, then tailored their presentations to the commander. By most accounts, this system worked well because the commander had his intelligence presented in the form he preferred, and Bletchley Park was kept

* The Bureau of Intelligence and Research provides relatively little support to line offices in the State Department structure; most of these offices rely on their own officers in the fields, e.g., the China Desk is usually more likely to seek information on conditions in Szechuan Province from the U.S. Embassy in Beijing rather than from the China analysts in INR. The impact of INR analysis depends largely on whatever influence the Director of INR has with the Secretary of State (it has varied under different administrations), and the INR staff supports the director in this capacity.

Some corporations have small "foreign risk assessment" offices, but most of these seem to suffer the same fate as INR; most are cut out of the policy loop, and most personnel consider them to be institutional backwaters. Those risk assessment offices that have been successful seem to be those whose members have been able to establish one-on-one relationships with individuals in the corporate hierarchy—much as some directors of INR have boosted their agency's stature by having a good working relationship with the Secretary of State. For example, William Hyland, who had worked with Henry Kissinger for many years on the National Security Council staff, later headed INR when Kissinger became Secretary of State and naturally had a close working relationship with the Secretary.

posted on the latest requirements from the field. This system also kept intelligence on a tight leash, as the SLU maintained control over the dissemination of their intelligence in the field. This was advantageous from a security standpoint.[26]

More recently, when George Bush was Director of Central Intelligence, he made a practice of letting analysts give presentations to high-level officials, up to and including the President. This may have reflected Bush's appreciation of the fact that he lacked the intelligence experience of such predecessors as Colby, Helms, and Dulles, but it also allowed the consumer to communicate directly with the analyst. In the give-and-take, the analyst would find out more about the specific concerns of the consumer and be better prepared to carry out the analysis. By most accounts, this practice also bolstered the morale of analysts, who believed they were making a meaningful contribution to policy.

Fortunately, modern secure communications and automated data processing are making face-to-face meetings between analysts and consumers and the production of tailored intelligence products easier. Today, for example, targeting staffs rely at least as much on informal contacts with the intelligence analysts responsible for covering the targets of interest as on finished publications. In this way, "intelligence production" often consists simply of the every-other-day conversations the targeteer has with the intelligence analyst on the secure telephone. Similarly, up-to-the-minute, tailor-made mission plans, including intelligence information on enemy forces, can now be produced for Air Force and Navy air crews using digital mapping data and graphic displays.

Placing intelligence analysts in or near the operational chain of command does run counter to traditional views of intelligence specialists. Most intelligence experts have argued that breaking down the walls that separate them from policymakers threatens an analyst's independence and his or her ability to be critical. Sherman Kent, for example, argued that unless analysts are kept outside the policy loop, they could be coopted by the officials they serve and become reluctant to produce estimates contrary to policies that have been adopted or appear likely to be adopted.²⁷ And an analyst who depends on his client for advancement in his career may be less willing to rock the boat by questioning the client's policies. As one of Kent's associates who himself later went on to chair the Board of National Estimates said: "If the policy-intelligence relationship is to work, there must be mutual respect, trust, civility, and also a certain distance. Intelligence people must provide honest and best judgments and avoid intrusion on policymaking or attempts to influence it. Policymakers must assume the integrity of the intelligence provided and avoid attempts to get materials suited to their tastes."²⁸

Nevertheless, even though there is some possibility that analysts who are included in the day-to-day operations of an organization may be coopted, they are also more likely to be aware of the current needs of the organization for intelligence. Similarly, although one could argue that intelligence officers in the chain of command may become reluctant to offer analysis that would undercut current policy because this would harm their chances for promotion, one could also argue that intelligence officers who depend on their clients for promotion decisions also have a great incentive to make sure their consumers are well-informed.

Finally, experience suggests that officials are more likely to accept intelligence from "one of the boys" rather than from outside "intelligence experts," who may be suspected of having hidden a policy agenda in the analysis. This is probably especially true when the intelligence news is bad. An Army official is more likely to listen to an Army intelligence analyst who tells him that Soviet weapons can pierce the armor of his new tank rather than to a CIA official who is suspected of wanting to prove once and for all that tanks are obsolete.

Thus, responsive intelligence and detached objectivity often present a straight trade of one for the other, and probably no compromise of the two objectives will ever be perfect, just as the compromise between ensuring responsive intelligence and protecting sources and methods will never be perfectly resolved. The best practical mix seems to be to minimize the distance between the analyst and the consumer and the analyst and the collection planner as much as possible, while also developing the professionalism among intelligence personnel necessary to ensure that intelligence judgments remain independent of policy considerations. Even so, the machine and its operation is bound to go awry even with the best personnel at the controls.

THREE

Intelligence and Collection

Some of the most dramatic changes in intelligence in recent years are the developments that have taken place in intelligence collection. Unfortunately, with this capability comes complexity, and with complexity comes new challenges.

This chapter explains how U.S. intelligence collection has evolved and discusses some of the challenges the intelligence community now faces. Of course, specific capabilities of U.S. collection systems must be kept secret—especially details concerning which approaches have been exploited and the degree to which they have been developed—but, fortunately, it is still possible to discuss collection in enough detail to understand the problems the community is encountering in collection planning.*

PROGRESS IN INTELLIGENCE COLLECTION

Most methods of intelligence collection are not radically different from those of forty years ago. The main difference is

* This chapter deals primarily with developments that have occurred in methods of collecting secret intelligence information. However, similar trends have been underway in the collection and processing of open-source data. For example, just as telecommunications have yielded favorable targets for SIGINT systems, intelligence analysts have also been able to take advantage of the spread of publishing, broadcasting, and news services throughout the world. Cable services such as AP, UPI, and Reuters reach into even the most remote spots in the world. Even television networks, using new miniaturized equipment, are able to cover distant events quickly. Although the Western media have had difficulty in covering some events because of local restrictions (e.g., the Iran-Iraq War and the Soviet intervention in Afghanistan), this been partially offset by the proliferation of new national broadcasting services; it seems that one of the first things a new country does upon receiving independence is to establish Radio Harare or Radio Comoros Islands, and these can be easily monitored.

capability. Almost all current collection systems, for example, fit into one of the three traditional collection disciplines, namely, human intelligence collection (HUMINT), signals intelligence (SIGINT), and imagery. Indeed, most collection systems now in use can trace at least one ancestor to the progress made under the pressure of World War II.

Consider SIGINT, for example. By 1945, SIGINT specialists developed early versions of most current SIGINT technologies, including automated frequency search devices, signal direction-finding systems, and—possibly most important—computer-assisted cryptography. Indeed, the "Bombe," which had been developed during the war by the British Secret Intelligence Service to break the German Enigma code, was one of the very first electronic computers. American and British specialists had also developed techniques such as "traffic analysis" (detecting an opponent's plans from the volume and pattern of messages in a communications network rather than their contents) and technical SIGINT (the analysis of enemy weapon systems by their emitted signals).[1] Similarly, the United States had developed the basic techniques of human collection via the network of sources the OSS operated during World War II—mainly in neutral countries such as Switzerland, Sweden, and Spain—and the RAF and the U.S. Army Air Corps had flown countless photoreconnaissance missions.[2]

The main problem for the United States in 1947 was that many of its wartime capabilities had been allowed to wither away or were unsuited for the new intelligence targets of the Cold War which, of course, were primarily in the Soviet Union. Most apparent was the decline that had taken place in U.S. human collection capabilities. The OSS had run an extensive network of agents during World War II, but the network had been demobilized and, even so, it would have been poorly suited to the Soviet target in any case. While OSS Director William Donovan was wary of Soviet postwar plans, the Axis powers were the immediate threat and the most pressing intelligence target, so relatively little effort was spent in developing sources on the Soviet Union. About the only favorable factors were the flow of emigrés and displaced persons from the Soviet bloc in the years following the war and some HUMINT assets inherited from the Germans.[3] U.S. postwar imagery capabilities were almost as meager. Imagery of the Soviet Union in the early days of the Cold War was so scarce that the British government authorities asked travelers for tourist photos they had taken when visiting Soviet bloc countries, and the U.S. Air Force sometimes depended on Tsarist-era maps and captured German reconnaissance photographs to plan bombing missions over the Soviet Union. Entire industrial cities had been built east of the Urals during the war on which the United States had no imagery.[4] The situation is, of course, much better today, but it is important to remember how far the intelligence community has had to come in forty years.

Platforms, Vehicles, Tradecraft

Intelligence collection is logically divided into two parts: getting to the target, and gathering the information once one gains access.

Probably the single most important development in gaining access to intelligence targets during the postwar period is the use of satellites. Satellites are used to perform a variety of intelligence missions, including imagery collection, SIGINT collection, communications, early warning, and others.[5] The U.S. intelligence satellite program illustrates how intelligence technology remains at—or well ahead of—the leading edge of technology in the "white world" (as opposed to the "black world," as the field of secret intelligence or military technology is sometimes called). The intelligence community began to consider proposals for reconnaissance satellites almost ten years before Sputnik I, and the earliest U.S. prototype photoreconnaissance satellite was "flown" just a little over a year after the first U.S. satellite, *Explorer I*, was placed in orbit.[6]

Yet spacecraft, of course, are not the only "platforms" from which intelligence is collected. The intelligence community also operates a variety of aircraft, ships, and ground stations. Some examples that have been discussed publicly include:

— Aircraft. In the early years of the Cold War, the intelligence community used converted bombers for reconnaissance missions. The United States periodically overflew the Soviet Union with modified B-36s and B-47s, for example, and some of the earliest photographs of the Soviet missile test facility at Kapustin Yar were obtained by the British using a Canberra bomber.[7] Later aircraft, such as the U-2 and SR-71, were specially designed for reconnaissance over hostile territory. The advanced technology used in some of these aircraft is reflected in the longevity of the U-2, which was developed more than thirty years ago and still holds the altitude record for single-engine airplanes. Similarly, the SR-71, first flown in 1963, is still the fastest operational aircraft. Aircraft used in less hostile environments, such as offshore monitoring of SIGINT, are usually modified cargo aircraft or airliners, e.g., the RC-135, which is a military version of a Boeing 707.[8]

— Ships, such as the converted Liberty ships formerly operated by the United States to collect ELINT. One, the U.S.S. *Liberty*, was attacked by Israel in the 1967 June War. Another, the U.S.S. *Pueblo*, was seized by North Korea in 1968. Currently such offshore monitoring is generally carried out by operational U.S. Navy warships. Today the United States also uses ships to monitor Soviet missile tests, as in the case of the COBRA JUDY radar system operated aboard the U.S.N.S. *Observation Island*. The community has also used specially designed ships to collect debris that may have intelligence value. The best-known example was *Glomar Explorer*, used to salvage a Soviet submarine that had sunk in the Pacific.[9]

— Ground sites, the most obvious of which are CIA stations in certain U.S. embassies, but also specialized sites such as the stations the United States operated in Iran to collect telemetry from Soviet missile tests.[10]

Sometimes the solution to getting into position to collect intelligence can be as challenging as the collection itself. This is obvious in the case with spacecraft, of course, but should not be underestimated in other cases. For example, some of the more interesting earthbound approaches to collection have been telemetry-intercept stations in the Caucasus Mountains of Iran, large phased-array radar systems in the Aleutian Islands, and a tunnel bored under the Berlin Wall to tap Soviet bloc landlines. Sometimes the solution is a Mach-3, high-altitude aircraft for collecting electronic emissions. Sometimes the solution is a small, quiet aircraft for collecting soil samples to determine whether a particular site in Iran was suitable for a landing strip prior to the attempted rescue of the American hostages in 1980.[11]

Once access is acquired, the intelligence must actually be collected. The current range of collectors used in the three disciplines includes imagery, signals intelligence and other nonimaging collection, and human intelligence.

Imagery. A recent exhibit on aerial reconnaissance at the Smithsonian Institution illustrated the range of technologies that are possible for satellite and aircraft imaging systems. The exhibit, which even included a restored U-2 hung from the ceiling, demonstrated high-altitude cameras, some of which were film systems, others of which were electro-optical systems that transmit imagery to ground stations via an electronic communication link (the particular systems shown had been used on the civilian LANDSAT earth resources survey satellite). The exhibit also provided samples of other kinds of imagery, including false-color imagery, or photographs taken through special filters to highlight, say, crop yields and production; infrared imagery, consisting of pictures produced through the heat waves that lie beyond the visible light spectrum; and synthetic-aperture radar, a system that produces pictures by bouncing microwaves off the earth and processing the reflected signal.[12]

Signals intelligence and other nonimaging collection. SIGINT originally consisted of message intercepts and little more. Today, in contrast, it is derived from almost every kind of electromagnetic emission that produces an identifiable signature. Moreover, sensors are also used to detect "natural emissions" (that is, electromagnetic phenomena other than transmitted signals) that have intelligence value. Some of the various forms of SIGINT include:

— COMINT, or communications intelligence. COMINT includes intercepted transmissions and can theoretically include voice, video, Morse, or even facsimile messages. Assuming access is possible, COMINT can be collected from the air waves, cables, fiber optics, or any other medium, and can include coded or uncoded messages.

— ELINT, or electronic intelligence. ELINT includes the intercept and analysis of noncommunication transmissions such as radar; this is a development of the early work done in this field by the British during World War II. Analyzing the emissions of a fire control radar, for example, enables an analyst to infer the capabilities of the gun or missile associated with the radar. Also, simply identifying the location of a radar is itself useful, as these indicate the location of certain enemy forces.[13]

— FISINT, or "Foreign Instrumentation Signals Intelligence." FISINT consists of intercepts of telemetry from an opponent's missiles or aircraft as they are being tested. Aircraft designers equip their test models with telemetry packages that relay data on the prototype's guidance system operation, fuel flow, staging, and other parameters. These data enable the system's designers to evaluate the performance of the prototype, but, if intercepted, they also allow an intelligence analyst to estimate the characteristics of the aircraft. One example of FISINT that became well-known to the general public is the telemetry taken from Soviet ICBM tests by United States.[14]

— LASINT, or intelligence collected via the analysis of laser and other directed-energy beams. No example of LASINT seems to have been publicly identified, though presumably such a system would be necessary to monitor, say, a laser communications system or a treaty banning the development of space-based laser weapons.

— RADINT, or information obtained by tracking an opponent's aircraft with radar. RADINT provides data both on the performance of the vehicle by analyzing the flight path and some of the physical characteristics of the vehicle itself by analyzing the reflected radar signal. One example is the COBRA DANE radar facility operated by the United States in the Aleutians, which is used to analyze Soviet missile tests impacting on Kamchatka Peninsula. As opposed to ELINT, which is obtained by analyzing an opponent's radar emissions, RADINT requires active scanning by the observer.[15]

— IRINT, or intelligence obtained by collecting infrared emissions, electromagnetic phenomena with wavelengths longer than those in the visible spectrum.* An

---

* IRINT is a good example of the ambiguity between imagery and SIGINT. IRINT collectors are often identified in the public literature as systems permitting one to "see in the dark," which would technically make them a form of imagery. Aside from some tactical visual systems for night flying and ground combat, the only IRINT systems that have been publicly identified are nonimaging systems. Examples of these include the early-warning satellites used to detect the presence and signature of a missile plume, which makes these satellites SIGINT systems rather than imaging systems.

A similar overlap can occur in the case of RADINT. It is technically feasible to produce imagery by radar, as the synthetic aperture radar used on the Space Shuttle demonstrated, and even ordinary radar is capable of making some metric analysis of a distant object (e.g., the often-quoted statement that U.S. early-warning radar can detect an object the "size of a basketball" in

example of IRINT is the early-warning satellites used by the United States to detect the launch of Soviet ballistic missiles. As a missile breaks through the atmosphere, IR sensors on the satellite detect the missile's plume.[16]

— NUCINT, or "nuclear intelligence," information obtained via the collection of radioactive materials, emissions, or debris. One primitive example was the first U.S. atomic monitoring system, which alerted the West of the first Soviet nuclear test in 1949 by detecting the resulting fallout cloud as it passed off the Soviet mainland into the Pacific Ocean. Analysis of nuclear debris also permits estimates of the design and yield of nuclear weapons. A more recent example of NUCINT was the Vela nuclear explosion detection system, used to monitor the Non-Proliferation and Partial Test Ban Treaties; the Vela was designed to detect the characteristic flash of a nuclear explosion.[17]

The Soviets, as one might expect, have their own versions of most of these systems; just as we fly RC-135s off Kamchatka, the Soviets fly TU-95s out of Cuba to collect SIGINT from U.S. naval installations along the East Coast. Generally, the Soviets operate less sophisticated systems but in larger numbers. So, for instance, while the United States might operate a single reconnaissance satellite for months or years, the Soviet Union will use and replace several satellites, each for a few days or weeks. Even so, the Soviet Union has proven that, where necessary, it can also build advanced technical collection systems. For example, the Soviets have developed a nuclear-powered, nonimaging radar satellite (RORSAT) for tracking U.S. naval units; no comparable U.S. system has been disclosed publicly, though there are frequent references in the press to proposed "space-based radar" systems. Also, the Soviets use about half of their manned Salyut space stations to carry out

---

space). However, the primary objective of radar systems at this time is detection and tracking, which is why we discuss it under the heading of SIGINT.

military and intelligence missions, a space system to which the United States has no counterpart.

Human intelligence. HUMINT capabilities have also progressed greatly during the postwar era. To the public, "HUMINT" remains synonymous with "spying," or clandestine activities, yet, in reality, overt collection operators such as State Department foreign service officers and military attachés still provide the bulk of HUMINT. Indeed, foreign service officers alone produce eight-tenths of all human reporting, according to some official reports. Whereas the United States in 1945 had embassies and consulates in Europe, the Americas, and a few Asian countries, today we maintain representatives in most countries around the world, including the many new states that have been created in Africa, the Middle East, and East Asia. All of these legations provide information for U.S. intelligence analysts.

There are other, semicovert sources of human intelligence as well, such as emigrés, displaced persons, and contacts from abroad. Admittedly, these sources grow stale from the moment they leave their homelands, and the flow of emigrés and refugees can vary greatly, depending on the emigration policies of other countries. Still, emigré reporting has been critical in estimating everything from living conditions in Vietnam after 1975 to morale and efficiency within the Soviet armed forces. Finally, the ease of global travel has allowed scientists and technicians from countries around the world to interact with each other.

Ironically, though "human intelligence" and "technical intelligence" are often contrasted with each other, they are in fact intertwined. Many new technical aids have been developed to improve the collection of HUMINT. Project Pyramider, discussed earlier, is an example of the sophisticated support systems agents have available today. Some recent revelations suggest that the Soviets are equally innovative. One former KGB colonel, for example, has described a miniaturized radio capable of recording "burst" transmissions he used while covertly working in the United States.[18] Conversely, in many cases, operation of a technical system requires the use of HUMINT tradecraft. Special collection sensors are often required to be put in place by an agent, for example.

PROBLEMS AND CHOICES IN PLANNING COLLECTION

The modern wonders of collection can be a mixed blessing. Though they make possible intelligence that would otherwise be unobtainable, they can also greatly increase the difficulty of planning. Indeed, during the past four decades, some of the most important controversies concerning the effectiveness of U.S. intelligence have hinged on collection issues.

What Is the "Best Mix?"

The intelligence community has only a limited amount of money to spend on collection, so inevitably one question concerning collection is what kinds of systems the community should buy—for example, should the United States invest heavily in SIGINT at the expense of imagery, imagery instead of HUMINT, and so on.

This issue is often badly misunderstood in public debates concerning intelligence policy. For instance, one of the most frequent criticisms of U.S. intelligence during the past several years is the claim by some observers that the intelligence community depends too much on technical collection such as SIGINT and imagery and pays too little attention to traditional human collection.

For example, Ray Cline, a former high-ranking intelligence official, has written that a critical failing of Stansfield Turner was that he neglected human collection while Director of Central Intelligence: "He [Turner] understood and managed technical intelligence systems efficiently, but photography and electronic signals could not reveal what was going on in men's minds. Espionage is desperately needed to fill gaps in our knowledge of foreign governments' intentions and the danger to U.S. interests in complex revolutionary situations like Iran and the Caribbean. From his record as DCI, it is clear that Turner had little feeling for agent collection."[19]

Most often, critics who say that the intelligence community stresses technical collection too much make two arguments. First, they claim that, while technical intelligence is good for such "bean counting" as tallying missile silos the Soviets have already built, it does not reveal such enemy intentions as how many silos the Soviets *plan* to build. These critics claim human intelligence is needed for that. Second, they assert that HUMINT has suffered because too many resources were diverted to technical collection systems. Alas, both of these assertions concerning HUMINT rank among the great myths of intelligence and can be easily debunked by some common-sense thinking.

Consider the claim that overemphasis on technical collection has undercut U.S. HUMINT capabilities. In truth, it is unlikely that any HUMINT program has ever been starved because the money that could have gone to HUMINT has been diverted to SIGINT or imagery collection instead. Technical systems are so expensive in comparison to human intelligence collection sources that cutting HUMINT simply would not provide significant funds for improving technical systems. The price for just *one* high-resolution satellite photograph is about $1,800—or, to put it another way, the community could buy the annual services of a middle-grade intelligence officer for the cost of about a dozen photographs.[20] So, if the intelligence community lacks HUMINT, it can be for a number of reasons—lack of access to targets, lack of suitable personnel, the lag that always occurs when shifting human assets from one target to another, simple neglect, and so on—but a decision to use the money saved from HUMINT for technical collection is not one of them.

Similarly, consider the argument that would seem to make the lack of HUMINT especially important, the argument which asserts that HUMINT is necessary for estimating plans and intentions. If true, it would seem that the U.S. intelligence community is being deprived of critical information. Yet, as it turns out, this argument is also incorrect.

Suppose, for example, an analyst wants to estimate Soviet ICBM deployments three years into the future. Given a choice, between, say, a HUMINT report describing firsthand a conversation in which the head of the Strategic Rocket Forces (SRF) said, "We will have 1,800 ICBMs deployed by the end of three years," and an imagery-based estimate of Soviet missile production capacity, an analyst would obviously rather have the HUMINT report. Though the estimate of production capacity would be useful in determining whether the Soviet official had realistic expectations, the overheard statement is unambiguous and authoritative. This is what critics of technical collection mean when they claim HUMINT is necessary to estimate intentions.

On the other hand, suppose the analyst had to choose between two other pieces of evidence. One item might be, say, a SIGINT report providing the transcript of an intercepted conversation between the head of the SRF and an aide, in which the SRF chief said at some point, "Good. Your actions will ensure we achieve our goal of 1,800 deployed ICBMs within three years." The other item might be a HUMINT report by a new source describing a conversation in which a Soviet colonel boasted that the Soviet Union would deploy "thousands and thousands" of ICBMs in response to U.S. strategic policies. Obviously the technical intelligence—the intercept—would be the more precise, more reliable indicator of Soviet intentions.

The tightly restricted Soviet party apparatus makes penetration difficult, and so most Soviet HUMINT will be, in the overwhelming number of cases, second-hand information. However, a number of factors indicate that the Soviets will continue to provide substantial numbers of SIGINT targets. For example, the geography of the Soviet Union requires that the Soviet government rely on various communication and broadcast systems to converse with the outlying provinces. The centralized structure of the Soviet bureaucracy suggests that the Soviets will rely on large-scale electronic information processing rather than microcomputers. Both facts mean that U.S. intelligence can count on a good number of Soviet SIGINT targets. Some will provide insight into Soviet intentions, and it is unlikely the Soviets will be able to protect or distort all transmissions.

Of course, the opposite might be true in a Third World country. Lacking much in the way of electronic communications, there may be few SIGINT opportunities, and so the best source of information—even for technical questions—may be a clandestine human source.

The lesson is that *how* information is acquired is a secondary point. The real issue is what *kind* of information is needed to answer a question. No one form of collection has an inherent advantage in answering a particular type of question. Which form of collection is best depends on the nature of the target, the particular data that are required, the opportunities that are available, and so on.

Ideally, one plans a mix of collection systems with three criteria in mind: making the most effective use of the funding that is available; covering the targets requested by intelligence consumers as effectively as possible; and deploying systems that complement each other. In a well-planned intelligence program, collection systems work together synergistically. Rather than using HUMINT against a fixed set of targets and SIGINT against others, the two should work in combination so that the total picture is more than just the sum of what is collected from each system.

When intelligence consumers say, "We need more HUMINT," they probably really mean that they want answers to such questions as "How active are terrorist groups going to be this year?" or "Is anyone plotting a coup to overthrow a Third World government friendly to the United States?" If technical collection systems have not provided the information necessary to answer these questions, it is easy to assume that *somewhere* there must be a knowledgeable insider who can be recruited. Yet, in truth, simply pouring money into HUMINT programs will not in itself improve intelligence. Planning human collection is as difficult as planning any other kind of intelligence.

A more important "best mix" issue in intelligence planning

is whether the intelligence community can adapt its collection strategies to respond to rapidly changing events. One such change, for instance, occurs when the target adopts counter-measures after it learns that the United States is collecting a particular type of intelligence. Once the Soviets learned the capabilities of U.S. reconnaissance satellites, for example, they resorted more to camouflage and nighttime deployments.[21] When this occurs, an intelligence planner faces a choice: should the intelligence community invest money to improve the existing collection systems, hoping to defeat the countermeasures, or should it shift to a different collection method?

One problem is that institutional bias will almost always favor the currently used approach, even when changing collection strategies might offer a bigger payoff. Not only would a new system require writing off investments and expertise developed for the existing system but it would also likely be opposed by the operators of the system, who are inevitably influential in the selection of new collection systems. These operators are likely to favor incremental improvements in existing systems rather than funding a new competitor. As a result, existing systems often have an advantage in the bureaucratic wars that occur when planning for intelligence.

Balancing Current Requirements
with Unexpected Demands in the Future

A second problem is how to provide the collection capacity needed for "routine" collection while also providing the flexibility needed to handle emergencies or unexpected developments.

Consider, for example, the question of "surge capacity." Collection planners are under pressure to eliminate waste so that as many targets can be covered as possible. But since the scope of intelligence is so broad, invariably there exists at least one consumer whose intelligence requirements are not being met adequately, and so it is always hard to justify holding back resources or maintaining redundant or back-up capacity. The choice is between preparing for some hypothetical future contingency or supporting the current requirements of a real intelligence consumer in the here-and-now.

Surge capacity means having six analysts when five could produce the same product; having two SIGINT processing facilities when only one is needed to meet the average daily demands; operating reconnaissance aircraft even when it is cheaper to cover the vast majority of targets with satellites; and so on. Moreover, total capacity is not the only issue. Surge capacity also requires extra flexibility: case officers must have a wide range of language skills; SIGINT systems must be designed to cover a broad range of frequencies. This flexibility is an additional hidden cost.

Hardly anyone would argue against surge capacity, but almost everyone in the budget process has a natural inclination to trim "excess" capability in their review of the intelligence budget. Congress and the executive branch are both under pressure to restrain government spending. Also, program managers of collection systems are generally evaluated according to their ability to respond to normal intelligence demands; the situations requiring surge capacity are relatively rare, and this gives program managers a natural incentive to concentrate their efforts on routine production.

Finally, the budget process is not designed to plan surge capacity effectively. Ideally, surge capacity can be planned for by finding the most critical "choke points" in all programs that contribute to carrying out a mission and then concentrating the resources allocated for surge capacity at those points. For example, if a satellite has the capability to produce one thousand images a day, but the ground processing facilities only have the capability to process four hundred images a day, then surge capacity depends completely on developing more processing facilities until their capabilities meet those of the satellite they serve.

Unfortunately, the "building blocks" of the intelligence budget, like most government agency budgets, are defined in reference to programs rather than intelligence missions (e.g.,

"Satellite Program A," "Aircraft Program B," and "Analysis Agency C," rather than "Providing intelligence to military units in the field," "Tracking Soviet mobile ICBMs," and "Monitoring narcotics trafficking"). As a result, the budget process usually does not provide an opportunity to focus on critical choke points or weak links. The weak links in the ability of the community to perform specific missions do not become clear.

Thus, in this example, it is entirely possible that the intelligence community would buy another satellite before it bought additional processing capability. Several legitimate reasons could be offered for doing so: an additional satellite, for example, could ensure the longevity of the program by keeping the satellite construction crew on hand. Unfortunately, specific choke points within the program, such as those just illustrated might be overlooked in the acquisition process and addressed only in the event of an intelligence failure.

The same problem applies to an issue related to surge capacity: survivability. The survivability of any collection system—its capability to operate even during natural disasters or war—is a matter of adding extra protection or redundancy to regular collection systems, or, alternatively, developing specialized back-up collection systems that are better suited to operating under adverse conditions. Either way, survivability comes at the expense of current capability. Adding protection or back-up components will inevitably detract from the optimal design of a collection system. Funding a specialized, survivable collection system will usually mean less money for systems used in routine collection.

Consider satellite survivability, for example. A recent study by the Office of Technology Assessment listed seven different possible measures for protecting satellites: hiding, deception, maneuver, hardening, electronic countermeasures, electro-optical countermeasures, and proliferation.[22] All of these measures would compromise the capability of a reconnaissance satellite, increase its cost, or both. Hardening a satellite, for example, invariably increases its weight, meaning that a

designer will have to use a more powerful launch vehicle, remove some collection equipment to make room for armor, or
operate the satellite in a lower-than-desired orbit. Alternatively, one could write off reconnaissance satellites for wartime use and assume imagery and SIGINT will be collected
through other means. If so, the intelligence community
would have to divert funds that would ordinarily be used for
satellites to these alternative systems.

DEALING WITH THE COMPLICATIONS OF TECHNOLOGY

The intelligence community's reliance on highly advanced
technical systems presents several new problems for intelligence.

Planning

Because modern collection systems take so long to develop,
design, and construct, ten to fifteen years may elapse from
the time the first concept studies for a system are undertaken
to the first deployment of the system. Once deployed, the system may remain operational for ten more years. Thus, in extreme cases, some of the systems that intelligence planners
are considering today will be operating in the year 2010! Obviously, anticipating the demands of intelligence consumers a
quarter century in advance is quite challenging.

Dependence on the Nonintelligence Base of Technology

The specialized "black world" technology of secret intelligence systems and "white world" technology that is known to
the public may often seem sharply separated by the wall of
security, but, in reality, the two are closely linked. One reason
is economies of scale. It would be prohibitively expensive, for
example, for the intelligence community to operate its own
independent space program, developing its own launch vehicles, operating its own launch facilities, and so on. Therefore, the intelligence community has traditionally "piggy-

backed" on the civilian NASA and Defense Department space programs. For example, when, in the early 1980s, NASA and DOD began to phase out its expendable launch vehicles (ELVs) and planned to depend solely on the space shuttle, intelligence satellites likewise had to be made compatible with the shuttle.[23]

Cost

Technical collection systems can be extraordinarily expensive. According to the Church Committee, the single largest item in the intelligence budget at the time it issued its report (1976) was the national SIGINT program. Since then, Scott Breckinridge, a former Deputy Inspector General of the CIA, has written that the rapid growth in intelligence space systems may have altered the balance somewhat.[24] Some idea of the expense of individual technical collection systems can be inferred from the fact that even a commercially available electro-optical satellite such as LANDSAT costs about $250 million, not including the additional $50 million required to launch the spacecraft into orbit via an expendable booster. A typical communications relay satellite costs about $100 million and requires $35 million for launching by the Space Shuttle. (LANDSAT uses technology similar to U.S. imaging satellites, and communications satellites use technology similar to that used in SIGINT collection satellites.)[25]

In general, the trend has been toward consolidation—in the case of satellites, for instance, a larger number of missions have been assigned to each individual system, and each system has consisted of a smaller number of individual satellites. Each satellite has been designed for greater endurance, further reducing the number of individual units. So, whereas a program may have previously consisted of thirty or forty relatively simple units, the more advanced program may consist of five or ten very sophisticated, highly capable—and very expensive—units. This, combined with the greater capability of each system, has raised the cost of each satellite.

The complications that result from the higher cost in capability of individual intelligence systems are similar to those encountered by defense analysts, who face an analogous problem as ships, tanks, and aircraft have increased in capability and price.[26] First, as the community buys fewer systems, some manufacturers will fail to receive contracts. Over the long run, this will reduce the number of manufacturers and the number of design teams able to develop new systems. As the productive base shrinks, the intelligence community will have less surge capacity. In an emergency, such as the outbreak of war or the catastrophic failure of a number of collection systems at once, the community will be less capable of responding with replacements because the necessary industrial base would have shrunk. The creative base for new ideas will shrink somewhat, too.[27]

Second, when the intelligence budget contains a relatively small number of expensive programs, the budget itself will become inflexible. Expanding intelligence programs to accommodate growing demands will require large blocks of money, which may be difficult to obtain. Similarly, any cuts in these systems would mean large losses in intelligence capabilities. So when intelligence systems become more expensive, adjustments in intelligence spending usually have to be borne by an increasingly smaller sector of the intelligence program.

And, third, a trend to smaller numbers of increasingly capable systems raises risks. As systems become more expensive and more complex, obviously it becomes less practical to have a "spare in the barn" or "in the pipeline" if a system malfunctions or is destroyed. The cost is too great, and often the parts are so difficult to build that it becomes physically impossible to deliver the systems more quickly or in large quantities.

If this is so, then, one might ask, why does the intelligence community continue to use increasingly complex systems?

One reason is that this technology is necessary as greater demands are placed on intelligence—as targets become more difficult to penetrate and more consumers demand a greater volume of intelligence. Again, this problem is analogous to a problem in defense: proponents of more sophisticated fighter aircraft, for example, say that this complexity is necessary to survive and win in battle.[28]

Another reason is simply that, as technology has become more abundant in society—e.g., communications, transportation, calculating—a greater number of technical intelligence targets have appeared. For instance, once countries such as Germany adopted long-distance coded telegraph communications to send messages to their embassies abroad countries such as Britain had an incentive to intercept and decode these messages. Similarly, as the banking and business communities became increasingly dependent on long-distance electronic transactions, intelligence services have had an incentive to develop the necessary equipment for tapping into satellite communication systems.

These reasons for relying more heavily on technology seem reasonable. Sometimes, though, intelligence technology is pushed to the limit—and beyond—by unrealistic intelligence requirements. For example, the United States currently targets Soviet missiles with its nuclear forces. The Soviets, however, are currently deploying mobile ICBMs. If we continue to require our military forces to target all Soviet ICBMs on a continual basis, the intelligence community would need systems capable of providing real-time, all-weather targeting information, which could be quite expensive.[29] The same applies to arms control monitoring: the United States currently can monitor the number of ICBMs the Soviets have deployed at any given moment, but the cost of capabilities for providing this same information at the same level of confidence when the Soviets deploy mobile missiles could be quite steep.

Intelligence funding—and especially funding for collection, which is often the most expensive part—will need to keep pace with the demands being presented to the intelligence community if these demands are to be met. But, as can also be seen, intelligence requirements must be considered part of the total package in evaluating any national security policy. For example, if the necessary intelligence is infeasible or too expensive, U.S. leaders might have to reconsider both its policy of targeting mobile ICBMs and the forces designed for that mission. Similarly, when U.S. officials develop an arms control proposal, they should first make sure that the necessary intelligence is feasible and affordable.[30]

All of these factors pose significant challenges for planning the collection necessary for strategic intelligence. It is clear that a necessary—but not sufficient—condition for meeting these challenges is a comprehensive assessment of intelligence requirements, matching them to the available resources, and considering the entire package of intelligence collection programs in the context of the country's overall national security policy.

Yet even perfect collection will fail to ensure security unless the information that is gathered is analyzed accurately and presented to intelligence consumers in a form responsive to their needs. How this can be done and the problems involved are the subjects of the next two chapters.

FOUR

The Analytical Process

Reduced to its essentials, intelligence analysis is the process of evaluating and transforming raw data into descriptions, explanations, and conclusions for intelligence consumers. Depending on the question a policymaker asks, analysis can take many forms, ranging from a simple report linking a Pakistani nuclear scientist with a program to build an atomic bomb, to a full-scale assessment of whether the Pakistanis will build an atomic bomb, when the bomb could be expected to be operational, and how the bomb would be initially deployed.

Unfortunately, while there are "how to" theories explaining foreign policy skills such as negotiation or warfare, there is no well-developed theory of how to produce intelligence analysis. Even in Sherman Kent's study, intelligence was treated simply as a "special category of knowledge," and most of *Strategic Intelligence* is devoted to illustrating that category of knowledge rather than explaining the theory and method of intelligence analysis.[1]

To our knowledge, no one has ever provided a cookbook method for producing strategic intelligence. One reason why there is no universal, systematic set of instructions outlining how to produce analysis or theory explaining when analysis is effective may be that intelligence topics are themselves too varied and too unpredictable. Another reason is that intelligence analysts themselves tend to be practical-minded people and are reluctant to embrace anything as abstract as a "theory" of their profession.

Even so, intelligence analysis is clearly a process of forming hypotheses, testing them with data, and integrating these findings into explanations, assessments, or predictions. This process follows many of the same rules as traditional theory building.[2] So, despite the reluctance of the typical analyst to think about work in these terms, it seems useful to think of an "analysis process" the same way one thinks of an "intelligence cycle"—as an idealized form that describes the steps an analyst follows in order to highlight the problems that can occur rather than to describe a precise set of procedures an analyst actually carries out in practice. In this chapter, we describe the process of analysis in general terms and discuss some of the problems of intelligence analysis from the perspective of the individual analyst—the "methodological" issues of intelligence. The next chapter describes some of the problems of managing and coordinating analysis in a large organization such as the intelligence community.

DEALING WITH INTELLIGENCE INFORMATION

The first step in producing intelligence analysis is to determine what information must be analyzed. For the purposes of intelligence, analysis requires dealing with four different types of "information" in preparing reports and estimates: known facts, secrets, disinformation, and mysteries. Indeed, in many respects analysis can be considered a process of providing consumers with known facts, uncovering secrets, identifying and discounting disinformation, and warning officials when intelligence—no matter how good—will be unable to resolve the mysteries they want answered.

Known Facts

For the purpose of intelligence analysis, known facts consist of information that can be collected from open sources and, at least in principle, can be determined with virtual certainty. These include basic geographic or economic data, such as those published by the United Nations or the Organization for Economic Cooperation and Development; documented official national policies and strategic doctrines that can be extracted from the media; estimates of a country's military capabilities prepared by private institutions, such as the International Institute of Strategic Studies; and data on the capabilities of warships, such as those published in *Jane's Fighting Ships*. For example, the official position of the Soviet delegation at the Geneva arms talks, a message broadcast over radio by the Ayatollah Khomeini to Mecca-bound Shi'ite pilgrims, and the current annual rice production of Burma are all known facts, or can be readily ascertained. Certain intelligence consumers require these data regularly—Treasury and Commerce Department officials, for example, need quarterly world trade statistics, and Department of Agriculture officials need current data on foreign crop production.

Requests for known facts are the easiest for the analyst to meet. While some analysis of raw data is almost always required, the main challenge to the intelligence analyst is to get these facts to the consumer quickly and in an appropriate format. Yet, though straightforward, maintaining a reliable data base of known facts is nevertheless important. Such facts provide much of the information on which estimates and forecasts are based. Also, known facts are usually important in establishing a benchmark against which new information is compared.

While known facts may not be especially difficult to obtain, they nevertheless can consume considerable resources, and this is a significant concern in an era in which the number of demands presented to the intelligence community is outpacing the resources made available to it and the intelligence budget is being stretched to the limit. Known facts—especially those concerning Western countries—can often be provided by the private sector, government agencies outside the intelligence community, or academia. Intelligence analysts have access to such private sector data bases, and, in principle, they should be able to direct their consumers to this information. Usually, though, the community is called upon to provide such information directly and, in the process, vouch for its validity and accuracy.

Indeed, despite the availability of public data bases, in recent years the intelligence community's responsibilities for providing "known facts" have tended to grow rather than shrink. Thirty years ago it was rare for the CIA or Defense Department intelligence services to release information to the public under their own identities, though sometimes the State Department would serve as the conduit for CIA information, as was the case in the publication of Khrushchev's famous "secret speech" denouncing Joseph Stalin to the CPSU Party Congress in 1956.[3] Today, in contrast, the intelligence community regularly produces certain data for the public.

For instance, the CIA's monthly publication on world oil and gas production levels is a standard reference in most large libraries, as is the CIA directory of Party and government officials in the Soviet Union and other Communist countries. The Department of Defense's annual, *Soviet Military Power*, which is prepared by DIA with contributions from other Defense Department intelligence services, is another example of a publicly available intelligence periodical, even though it often goes beyond the realm of "known facts" and presents what amount to declassified estimates of Soviet weapon systems and deployments. The same is true of "special reports" occasionally released by the CIA, such as its 1978 estimates of Soviet military spending, its 1980 report on Chinese defense spending, and the 1985 report by the CIA's Deputy Director for Intelligence and the National Intelligence Officer for Soviet Strategic Programs on trends in Soviet nuclear weapon deployments.[4]

Secrets

Secrets provide the analyst with information about issues, situations, and processes that are intended by foreign governments or groups not to be known. Usually facts are secret because organizations take steps to keep them that way. This information can range from highly protected secrets such as the membership of a terrorist group or the performance envelope of a foreign military aircraft, to such simple statistics that certain governments do not choose to publish such as gold export figures from the Soviet Union or census data from the People's Republic of China.

Developing an assessment based on secret information requires two tasks, roughly analogous to estimating a mean and variance in statistics. Intelligence analysis involving secrets requires information that can often be obtained only through spies, exotic technical collection systems, or the piecing together of various fragments of open-source data thought to reflect secret information. All secret information invariably contains gaps and ambiguities. Therefore, the first task for the analyst is to determine a single best estimate. The second is to identify the range of uncertainty associated with such an estimate and reduce it if possible.

Assumptions and best estimates. Assuming two analysts have access to the same data, most of their disagreements on an estimate will be a result of the fact that each is working from a different set of assumptions. Such a situation occurred, for example, during the late 1970s when U.S. analysts were assessing future Soviet military production.

At the time, the United States was considering various alternatives for modernizing its armed forces, including new strategic nuclear weapons, such as the MX missile and various kinds of cruise missiles, new armored vehicles, such as the M-1 Abrams tank and M-2/3 Bradley armored fighting vehicle, and new warships. Yet, at the same time, several arms control agreements were being negotiated: SALT II, the Mutual and Balanced Force Reduction (MBFR) talks for conventional weapons in Europe, the Threshold Nuclear Test Ban Treaty, and others. One factor shaping the views of U.S. officials on these policies was the effect they would have on Soviet actions.

Some analysts believed that U.S. policies would influence Soviet military planning. They argued that the U.S. buildup would cause the Soviets to accelerate some of their defense programs, while arms control treaties would lead them to curtail others. Other analysts believed that the U.S. buildup and arms control would have only a minor effect on Soviet military deployments. They argued that Soviet deployments would mainly hold to their existing pattern because the Five-

Year Plan for the Soviet economy, which was being formulated at the time, would constrain Soviet choices.[5] The Soviets might chaff at U.S. policies, these analysts said, but they would be unable to do much more than complain, since the Soviet defense program was locked into the Five-Year Plan.

Although few intelligence analysts would refer to anything as academic-sounding as "a theoretical disagreement," this is precisely the reason why two analysts would disagree on this question. In this case, the theoretical disagreement was over how the secret Soviet military planning system operates. The first view, which concluded that the Soviet Union would respond to U.S. deployments and arms control agreements, was, in fact, using concepts from a traditional "nation-state" model of international politics. It assumed—at least implicitly—that the Soviet Union would behave as any rational player would and react predictably to outside events. The second point of view, which concluded that the Soviets could not respond because they were constrained by the Five-Year Plan, was using concepts from classical organization theory, such as that pioneered by Herbert Simon. It assumed that, even though Soviet officials might want to respond to events by changing their plans, they could not and would not because of the constraints imposed by the Soviet bureaucracy.[6]

The objective in intelligence, of course, is not to perfect theories. Nevertheless, it would have been impossible to choose one of these assessments over the other without understanding the logic and assumptions—that is, the theory—underlying each. Both assessments had some support from hard data. The Soviets do seem to pay considerable attention to arms control provisions in their military plans for research, development, and production, but it is also true that extraordinary effort can be required to change the Five-Year Plan. Collecting additional information could have settled this disagreement, but *only* if it addressed the underlying assumptions of the two theoretical explanations. In other words, the analysts would have to determine whether Soviet leaders are united enough to respond to a U.S. buildup, how rigid the Soviet economic planning process really is, or both. These factors are, at least in part, secrets. Notice, too, that neither of these questions has much to do with arms control or Soviet military policy per se, but until these issues are settled one cannot make an informed choice between the two assessments.[7]

Once one thinks of disagreements among analysts as arguments over "theoretical assumptions," it is easier to sympathize with the challenges intelligence analysis poses. For example, consider the often-cited case of the intelligence community's underestimates of Soviet ICBMs during the 1960s. After the intelligence community overestimated Soviet ICBM deployments in the late 1950s and early 1960s, CIA and State Department intelligence analysts assumed that the Soviet Union would deploy just enough strategic nuclear weapons for a "minimal deterrent," or just enough to threaten U.S. cities with nuclear retaliation. These analysts appear to have based their analysis on concepts of strategic deterrence accepted at the time in many American circles, believing that the Soviets would also appreciate the logic of this thinking and would act accordingly. These analysts were later proved wrong. Apparently the Soviets did not accept the prerequisites for deterrence then accepted by some Western thinkers, and these analysts have been roundly criticized over the years for slavishly "mirror imaging" Soviet behavior.*

But "mirror imaging" *can* be a valid assumption, and, ironically, it *would* have been a reasonably valid assumption in this instance if the U.S. analysts had, instead of using the logic of U.S. diplomatic postures or views provided for public consumption, used the logic of U.S. military policy.

It is true that the publicly stated policy for strategic deterrence that most U.S. officials presented in the 1960s followed

* "Mirror imaging" is the term some critics of U.S. intelligence often use to describe the alleged tendency of U.S. analysts to ascribe American values, perceptions, or motives to the Soviet Union or some other adversary. Aside from being an awkward use of a noun as a verb, it also happens to be a misnomer, since in a mirror the "image" on the other side of the looking glass is reversed, while the writers who coined the term intended to say that the image would react and plan the same way the United States would.

the logic of deterrence popular in American academic circles and think tanks. According to this logic, nuclear weapons had no real military value and were good only as a deterrent against a Soviet nuclear attack. To ensure deterrence, the logic went, the United States should deploy nuclear forces that could always retaliate after a Soviet attack but were not capable of disarming the Soviets, lest the Soviet leadership be provoked into launching a preemptive strike. Therefore the U.S. policy presented to the public by civilian officials was to develop survivable strategic weapons, deploy just enough of these weapons for a credible retaliatory force, and avoid developing weapons that might appear capable of disarming the Soviet Union with a so-called "first-strike capability."

However, U.S. military operational planning was not firmly bound by this policy and sometimes followed its own course. The U.S. military community based its plans on an operational doctrine that aimed at the destruction of the Soviet Union's total war-making capabilities: military bases, defense industries, nuclear weapons, and so on. This doctrine was an offshoot of the principles of strategic bombing originally articulated by Giulio Douhet in the 1920s and refined by the United States and Great Britain during bombing operations against Germany and Japan in World War II. These operational plans had a considerable influence on the types and numbers of strategic weapons the United States deployed. For example, the Air Force based its requests for missiles and bombers on the number of warheads it needed to meet its targeting requirements.[8]

As it turned out, the operational doctrine of the Soviet Strategic Rocket Forces (and, presumably, its force structure) was similar to the operational plans of the U.S. military. The guidelines described by Soviet military writers for targeting strategic nuclear forces read remarkably like those of U.S. military writers. For example, former Chief of the Soviet General Staff V. D. Sokolovskii, in his opus *Military Strategy*, wrote that the objectives of the Strategic Rocket Forces were to destroy the war-making capability of the enemy, meaning, in order of priority, its nuclear forces, its political and military command system, and its war industries. These objectives and priorities were virtually identical to those used by U.S. targeteers.[9]

So understanding how the Strategic Air Command targeted the Soviet Union and planned its force structure would have been a good starting point from which to estimate the plans of the Soviet Strategic Rocket Forces—critics of "mirror imaging" not withstanding. Unfortunately, with the exception of the Air Force analysts who had worked with SAC, most U.S. intelligence analysts were not intimately familiar with U.S. operational plans for strategic war. (As it turned out, the Air Force produced the most accurate forecasts of Soviet missile deployments during this time.)

In other words, "mirror imaging" can be a valid analytic technique. The issue is not mirror imaging per se—or "assuming rationality" on the part of leaders such as Qaddafi or Khomeini, resorting to stereotypes, and other supposed fallacies—but whether the assumptions implicit in the approach are valid. In this case, the critical question is whether Soviet military planning is aimed at the same objectives as U.S. military planning.

It is tempting to say that this kind of problem appears only in making political forecasts, which are traditionally "softer" than scientific and technical intelligence. ("You can't fudge physics.") Yet the same problem can occur just as easily in assessments of military hardware and forces. For example, at about the same time the debate over Soviet military planning described above was underway, there was also the debate cited earlier over the range of the Soviet TU-22M "Backfire" bomber. The disagreement occurred because the CIA and DIA used two different models, each developed with the assistance of a different contractor. Both models used hard data, such as telemetry, calculated drag coefficients, assessments of the efficiency of the Backfire's engines, and so on. The models differed, however, in their assumptions about certain aspects of how the Backfire would actually be operated, and this difference led the DIA to attribute considerably greater range to the aircraft than did their CIA counterparts.[10]

In other words, the Backfire disagreement was a "theoretical" problem similar to the one that led to the disagreement on Soviet responses to the U.S. program to rebuild its defenses and developments in arms control—a problem of determining the validity of underlying assumptions about secret information. In both cases, the solution depended on investigating the secondary questions underlying the disagreement. This was, in fact, done, and today there is little disagreement on the true operational range of the Backfire.[11]

Until such questions are resolved, the best that the intelligence analyst can do is to inform the intelligence consumer that the data plausibly support several different interpretations, and why. When two "truths" are plausible, the decision to be made is in reality a political choice and not a decision that can be based strictly on intelligence analysis.

Uncertainty. Uncertainty requires intelligence analysts to make probabilistic estimates and assessments, such as "it is highly likely," "it is unlikely," "it is highly unlikely," and so on. Sherman Kent went so far as to suggest arranging such expressions on an ordinal scale to express explicitly the probability associated with an event.

Policymakers are notorious for criticizing this kind of intelligence assessment. Just as domestic policy officials prefer one-handed economists, officials responsible for foreign policy prefer definitive intelligence analysts who will give them forecasts along the lines of "China *will* sign a trade agreement with Japan," or "the Communists *will not* come to power in Italy." It is easy to sympathize with these officials, as it does little good for an official to adopt a policy such as protective tariffs on Japanese imports because an intelligence estimate says that there is only a one-out-of-ten probability that the Japanese will retaliate, and then to see Japan indeed retaliate—an outcome entirely consistent with the estimate. Yet this is the only way analysis can be provided when there is uncertainty. It is not always possible to describe uncertainty as precise odds or even in standardized terminology, but such an estimate will nevertheless have to be expressed as a prediction with some recognized room for error.

For example, during the 1980/1981 Polish crisis, labor and social unrest threatened the Communist regime, and some Western observers suspected that the Soviets might invade the country, just as they had invaded Czechoslovakia in 1968 when the Dubchek government adopted policies that threatened Soviet control. According to press reports, the United States had some information suggesting that the Soviets had plans to carry out this threat. But there were also signs suggesting that the Soviets would not invade, and U.S. analysts knew that there were several specific factors that could not be estimated with any real degree of confidence but that were understood to be important to the Soviet decision. Sherman Kent called these "known unknowns," and in this case, they probably included Soviet confidence in the reliability of their forces and the Soviet estimates of the likelihood the Poles would resist.

As a result, the intelligence community could only indicate that, on balance, it was "unlikely" that the Soviets would invade, describe the amount of uncertainty in their estimate, and then identify the key factors that were responsible for this uncertainty. For example, if the uncertainty in their estimate of the likelihood of a Soviet invasion of Poland depended on the ability of the Soviets to find a suitable Quisling who would both cooperate with the Soviet Union and be able to maintain control over the Polish army, the Polish Communist Party, and the Polish population, then this had to be made explicit, along with any other factors that affect the level of uncertainty. The estimate then would have been able to go on to present the best information available about these factors and the effect that variations in these factors had on the estimate.

Though intelligence consumers want definitive answers, this is often impossible, and the best that can be done is to identify the sources of uncertainty and assist the consumer in understanding them. In the long run, this type of analysis improves intelligence, as it identifies the specific factors that require additional data or analysis to reduce future uncertainty.

Disinformation

Disinformation refers to "facts" that are the result of a conscious effort by the opponent to conceal, deceive, or mislead analysts. Deception has a long history in strategy. Most people are familiar with the tale of the Trojan Horse of Homer's *Iliad*, and many other examples come quickly to mind. One of the great espionage stories of World War II is Ewen Montagu's account of Operation Mincemeat and the "man who never was."

In this operation, Montagu and his colleagues in the British Secret Intelligence Service acquired a corpse, dressed him as a Royal Marine, and equipped him with an opened parachute, a life jacket, and a briefcase containing forged high-level correspondence between British military leaders. One letter referred to plans to fool the Germans into concluding that the next Allied objective would be an invasion of Sicily rather than some other unmentioned objective, which was the real target. The British then took the corpse, provided it with an ingeniously complete set of fabricated identity papers and personal effects identifying him as "Captain (Acting Major) William Martin, RMC," and set it adrift from a submarine off the coast of Spain. When the Spaniards recovered the body, the Franco government allowed German intelligence agents to photograph the documents before returning the corpse to the British. The Germans took the bait and redeployed some of their units to Corsica—thus reducing resistance to the invasion of Sicily, which had indeed been the real target all along.[12]

Many other cases of deception could also be cited, such as the non-existent army General George Patton was to lead in a D-Day invasion of Callais in a ruse to divert attention from Normandy, the real target; the *Wolnosc i Niepodlenosc*, a bogus Polish resistance group run by the Soviets in the early 1950s to draw out Polish dissidents and mislead Western intelligence services; and others.[13] Deception and disinformation has received much attention in the past few decades because, according to some analysts, they are major components—called "active measures"—of Soviet foreign policy initiatives. For example, these analysts point out, the Soviet General Staff has an entire directorate devoted to "strategic deception." A Soviet GRU defector who writes under the pseudonym "Viktor Suvorov" points out that Marshal N. V. Ogarkov, before becoming the Soviets' chief military representative at the SALT negotiations and Chief of the General Staff, was in charge of this directorate.[14] Similarly, the Senate Select Committee on Intelligence has published examples of counterfeit letters forged by the Soviets and intended to discredit the United States. One letter, for instance, purporting to be from the U.S. Information Agency to the Chairman of the Select Committee, contained instructions for the Select Committee to exaggerate the damage caused by the explosion of the Chernobyl nuclear power plant.[15]

The threat of disinformation, however, goes beyond the immediate danger of causing an intelligence assessment to go awry. Disinformation can also distort the victim's general confidence in its intelligence channels, in which case the credibility of many other assessments will be brought into question. Paradoxically, this damage usually occurs when disinformation is successfully exposed. For instance, one byproduct of the discovery of past Soviet deception campaigns has been to make some writers so preoccupied with disinformation that they exaggerate a genuine problem into a general indictment of the quality of U.S. intelligence. Also, intelligence failures are often attributed to disinformation even when there might be many other reasons of a more innocuous nature for the error.[16]

So, from the viewpoint of the intelligence analyst, disinformation really presents two separate problems: first, detecting when deception occurs to ensure the accuracy of a specific assessment, and, second, maintaining an accurate assessment of the reliability of sources in general.

Detecting deception usually occurs in one of two ways. The

first way is by discovering a deception operation directly when a new information source is acquired. An example of direct discovery occurred when Oleg Penkovskiy informed Western intelligence agencies in 1961 that the real cause of the death of Strategic Rocket Force Commander in Chief Mitrofan Nedelin in 1960 was the explosion of a rocket being prepared for launch at Tyuratam rather than an airplane accident, as reported by the Soviet press.[17] Such examples of uncovering deception, incidentally, illustrate how "positive" intelligence and other aspects of intelligence, such as counterintelligence, are intertwined.

The other way to determine that deception has occurred is by examining patterns of anomalies in intelligence. When deception is discovered in the process of analysis, it usually occurs gradually. First information is received that initially appears simply to be an anomaly, then a body of evidence counter to existing conclusions accumulates, and, finally, over time, a counterargument becomes compelling enough to set into motion a reappraisal that eventually overturns existing assessments. Detecting deception this way is usually a painful process, no matter how good the evidence, since few people enjoy questioning their existing opinions. As Leon Festinger and numerous cognitive psychologists who followed him have shown, most people will hold to their existing belief structure even in the face of considerable contrary evidence and will change their beliefs only after the accumulated evidence is both inescapable and intolerable. Experiments with individuals suggest that reaching a level of dissonance sufficient to change one's thinking is quite difficult.

For instance, in the late 1950s and early 1960s, Soviet leaders deliberately exaggerated the number of ICBMs the Soviet Union had deployed. Among the members of the U.S. intelligence community, the Air Force was the agency most willing to accept the Soviet statements, believing that the supporting evidence confirmed the Soviet claims. The deception was exposed when the first U.S. reconnaissance satellites proved that the Soviet Union had in fact deployed just a handful of SS-6s. Yet the Air Force analysts were extremely reluctant to retreat from their original estimates. Rather than simply accept the imagery evidence, the analysts went to great lengths to find the additional missiles they believed the Soviets had deployed. Since the Air Force analysts firmly believed that the available evidence indicated that the Soviets must have built large numbers of missiles, their first response was to hypothesize that the Soviets must have hidden them. According to one story (probably apocryphal), they even attempted to show that a missile had been hidden in an old castle.[18]

It is easy to criticize these analysts in retrospect, but no professional analyst would immediately discard an estimate believed to have been supported by the evidence up to then. Certainly the Air Force analysts were not unique in their determination to stick to their position. A similar situation occurred just before World War II, when Germany built the battleship *Bismarck*. Under the provisions of the Washington Treaty of 1922, battleships were limited in size to 35,000 tons (limiting displacement constrained the armor, firepower, and speed of a ship). In 1936, the Germans laid down the *Bismarck* in Hamburg. In compliance with the treaties then in effect, the same day the ship was started, the German Embassy in London informed the British government that the *Bismarck* would comply with the 35,000-ton limit and that the ship would be 792 feet long, 118 feet wide, and would mount 15-inch guns. These data were accurate, but the Germans lied about the draft, armor, and horsepower of the ship in order to make the ship's displacement appear to be within limits.

A few British naval analysts believed that the *Bismarck* was a treaty violation, but most apparently did not. One attaché, rather than considering that the ship might have a deeper draft than reported, decided that the *Bismarck* had been designed with an unusually shallow draft for waters of the Baltic and was therefore mainly intended to fight the Soviet Navy. Another British officer, who had taken part in naval negotiations with the Germans, was reluctant to question the reported dimensions of the *Bismarck* precisely because that would have meant Germany had violated the treaty. Indeed,

the British Navy's Intelligence Division did not alter its estimate even after the *Bismarck* was sunk and British analysts
had been able to examine the ship's log and interrogate its
surviving crew. The Admiralty continued to accept its intelligence service's estimate until a year later, when it received
incontrovertible information from Soviet intelligence clearly
indicating that the ship was, in fact, in violation.[19]

Most sociological and psychological evidence suggests that
the willingness to question existing dogma—an attitude essential for defeating such deception—is rare. Thomas Kuhn,
a leading student of the history of science, has noted that,
even in the supposedly coldly objective scientific community,
scientists usually do not change their theoretical views.
Rather, Kuhn writes, it is more common for scientific thought
to evolve as new scientists replace old scientists, rather than
for old scientists to change their existing beliefs. For instance,
alchemists did not become chemists; rather, chemists took
over as their ideas proved more useful and the alchemists
died off. The same is true of the political views most people
hold. As Voltaire observed, only a generation can change a
belief.

One might hope that organizations would compensate for
this tendency of individuals, but experience suggests that it
may be even more difficult for an organization to abandon its
existing beliefs, and especially an intelligence organization,
whose very reason for existence is to provide reliable information. Changing an intelligence estimate can undermine
the organization's reputation, and almost everyone within the
organization has an incentive to prevent that. Also, organizations have built-in defense mechanisms that protect the existing dogma, regardless of the accuracy of these beliefs. Individuals who criticize the organization's existing position
tend to be weeded out by the process of promotion and performance evaluations, (though, in practice, actual purging is
unnecessary, as dissenters can read the writing on the wall
and usually leave for greener pastures on their own accord).

In any case, uncovering deception is only half of an analyst's problem. The other half is maintaining an accurate as-

sessment of the reliability of intelligence sources. Part of the difficulty in doing so is that two types of errors are possible.

The more obvious threat is the possibility that an analyst will commit a "false positive"—accepting a source as valid when, in fact, it is being used as a channel for disinformation. This is the threat usually associated with disinformation and was what happened in the "missile gap" episode, when the U.S. intelligence community accepted the evidence—much of it official statements planted by leading Soviet officials—suggesting that the Soviets had embarked on a massive buildup of their long-range missile force.

The likelihood of "false positives" is in large part because information gaps are a routine intelligence problem. Analysts expect gaps in their understanding and thus "go with what they've got," using what information they have. It is to be expected that disinformation will fill the vacuum left by intelligence gaps, as there often is little or no valid information for evaluating these faulty data.

On the other hand, an analyst can also commit a "false negative"—rejecting a source when, in fact, it is a valid channel of information. In this case, an analyst becomes so suspicious of deception that he fails to use bona fide information. This was what happened when U.S. intelligence analysts discounted human-source reporting in mid-1962 suggesting that the Soviets were in the process of constructing intermediate-range missile sites in Cuba. In that instance, HUMINT was suspect in part because previously it had erroneously predicted that the U.S.-sponsored invasion at the Bay of Pigs would trigger a popular uprising against the Castro regime. Also, U.S. analysts knew that these reports came largely from Cuban exiles, who had an interest in inciting the United States to take strong action against Castro.

The all-time classic example of such caution taken to the extreme is almost certainly the case of Yuri Nosenko, a KGB officer who defected to the United States in June 1962. A few years before Nosenko's defection, CIA counterintelligence had discovered that it had been "burned" by failing to discover Kim Philby, a Soviet agent who had successfully penetrated British intelligence, and U.S. intelligence had been compromised when Philby took part in joint Anglo-American operations. A Soviet defector, Anatoli Golitsin, had helped expose Philby and thus gained stature as a source of counter-intelligence. Golitsin, alas, branded all Soviet defectors who escaped after he did as provocateurs trying to discredit him. One of these was Nosenko, who, as a result of his being suspected, was not only rejected as an intelligence source but also spent two-and-a-half years in confinement as U.S. intelligence attempted to "break" him.[20]

A final aspect of the disinformation problem is the tendency for an analyst to believe he has found a new intelligence development, when in fact the only thing "new" is more information being made available from better collection capabilities or, in some cases, increased attention to the subject. This appears to have occurred in 1979 when U.S. intelligence analysts thought that they had discovered a new Soviet combat brigade in Cuba. In truth, the Soviets had quietly deployed the brigade sometime in the early 1960s. Ordinarily, the Soviets do not announce deployments of combat units abroad, and they almost never announce the deployment of specific military units. Eventually the Soviet brigade was discovered and mistakenly identified by U.S. intelligence in the late 1960s as a Cuban unit. When additional intelligence became available in 1979, U.S. analysts correctly detected the Soviet unit, but they did not immediately realize that this unit was the same one that had been mistakenly identified as Cuban ten years earlier. The result was a major flap between the Soviet Union and the United States.[21]

This problem is especially apt to occur during crises, when events redirect the attention of the analyst to phenomena that may have been present for some time but that had simply gone unnoticed. It is also likely to occur with the introduction of better collection capabilities. In either case, it is exaggerated by turnovers in personnel, reorganizations, and other events that upset the continuity of an analytic organization.

Mysteries

Mysteries are just that: questions or issues that no amount of intelligence analysis or collection of secret information will reveal. Mysteries occur when all the information—known and secret—still cannot determine a most likely estimate, or cannot determine which of two or more estimates is more likely.

The reason why mysteries are insoluble is not simply a lack of information but often the nature of the question being posed. For example, a question is a mystery when it can be demonstrated that more than one outcome is logically possible and equally probable. It may be theoretically possible to limit the number of possible outcomes, but one would require information that is, in principle, unlikely to be obtained. One illustration of how a mystery can be created, for example, is what is known as the "voter's paradox," a situation originally identified by the economist Duncan Black and later elaborated by Kenneth Arrow.[22]

Assume an intelligence analyst is asked to predict the decision that the cabinet of a foreign government might make on economic policy. To simplify the illustration, assume further that there are three policies under consideration—policies A, B, and C—and that the cabinet is comprised of three members, all having one equal vote and each having the following preferences for the policies being considered:

> Minister #1 prefers Policy A most, B next, and C least;
> Minister #2 prefers Policy B most, C next, and A least; and
> Minister #3 prefers Policy C most, A next, and B least.

Finally, assume that the decision-making procedure for the cabinet is to vote on pairs of alternatives, with the winner facing the remaining alternative in a runoff.

In the situation described here, when the cabinet votes, it will be unable to produce a clear winner. In a straight vote, Policy A would defeat B (by the votes of ministers 1 and 3, both of whom prefer A to B), Policy B would defeat C (by the votes of ministers 1 and 2), and Policy C would defeat A (by the votes of ministers 2 and 3). As a result, it is impossible to know which policy will finally be adopted without knowing how, at that particular meeting, the votes are arranged in order; whether more than one runoff vote is allowed and, if so, how and when the process will be terminated; whether issues other than the three policies being considered at the meeting affect the voting; and so on. The ministers themselves may not know the answers to these questions until they arrive at the meeting, sense its dynamics, and begin to negotiate with their colleagues.

Of course, this is a highly contrived example, but it is presented as such in order to make clear that in some political situations, it is simply not possible to predict the outcome, other than to say that any one of several possible outcomes is equally likely to occur. In this case, even if a U.S. agent were at the meeting itself, he might not be able to predict the outcome until the instant it happened. So, in this particular case, the outcome of the policy process is a mystery.

But it is not only political events that lend themselves to mysteries. Suppose, for example, that an intelligence analyst were tasked to predict the flip of a fair coin. He could report that there is a 50 percent probability of the coin landing "heads" and an equal probability of it landing "tails," but, assuming the coin is indeed fair, no amount of analysis or information—chemical analysis of the coin's composition, aerodynamic modeling, radar analysis of the coin's trajectory, etc.—would enable him to predict the outcome of a single trial.

This problem of questions that are insoluble in principle is actually quite common in most scientific or scholarly enterprises and has received greater recognition in recent years. For instance, twenty years ago many meteorologists would have thought that, if enough information and sufficiently powerful computers were available, then, at least in principle, the weather could be predicted several months in advance. Today most meteorologists would not hold this view, because they know that even though their models and theories may be correct, they still may not know about or be able to collect enough information on essential factors that will determine the weather. The result is not that meteorologists no longer make forecasts. Indeed, meteorologists today forecast weather conditions further into the future than before. The difference is that they are more careful to acknowledge just what kinds of forecasts they are unable to make.[23]

Strictly speaking, it would seem as though most mysteries are really incompletely understood secrets and that, with an unlimited amount of effort, even mysteries could be solved. For instance, in the real world there is no such thing as a perfectly fair coin; there are minute factors that do bias the result, and, with enough effort, the effect of these factors should be measurable and, hence, predictable.

The question is one of selecting the most useful conception of reality for the purposes of explanation and prediction. The conditions necessary for a voting cycle, a fair coin, a perfect vacuum, or a frictionless plane may never be perfectly attained, but they still may be the most valid representation— or at least a more valid set of assumptions than any available alternative.

Political questions having no definitive answers are easiest to illustrate in small, simple situations, such as cabinet meetings or games of chance, but the same kinds of insoluble puzzles can also occur on a larger scale. For example, during the mid- and late-1970s, a question often presented to the intelligence community was, "What are Soviet global intentions?" The question really referred to whether the Soviets would initiate confrontational policies in Europe and the Third World, and, indeed, several full-blown, interagency studies and NIEs were written to respond to this question. Yet, in fact, this question was probably a mystery. There were too many unknowable factors implicit in the question, and a number of Soviet decisions were logically possible, even assuming that all factors affecting Soviet decisions were understood. The actions of the Soviet Union depended on internal political developments, the interests of particular ministries or factions within the Soviet government, and social and demographic factors.

Often the source of an intelligence mystery is a question that is overly vague or poorly defined, as, for example, when officials submit broad questions (such as "Is the Soviet leadership expansionist?") and expect them to be used to predict specific actions (such as "Will the Soviets attempt to install a puppet regime in Country X?"). The futility of attempting such an analysis can be appreciated by asking the same question about U.S. global intentions. An analyst could offer some generalities: protecting governments favorable to the United States, and especially NATO, Japan, and Israel; maintaining free trade; supporting human rights where possible; and so on. But how do these judgments translate into a useful intelligence estimate? Just how strong is the U.S. commitment to NATO? What specific actions would it undertake to protect its allies? Under what conditions, if any, would it sacrifice its good relations with Japan for the sake of Israel's well being?

It is unlikely that large organizations such as the Soviet Union have "intentions," except in a very broad sense that does not facilitate any meaningful predictions. This, of course, does not deter officials from asking unanswerable questions or requesting predictions about events that are in reality mysteries. The problem mysteries pose to the intelligence analyst is that government officials often expect answers to them, when no answer is possible and the analyst has to say so. In truth, the analyst's best response—though often impolitic—is to help the intelligence consumer reframe the question so that some useful information can be provided.

Mysteries help define the boundary between intelligence and policy. The intelligence community's goal is to assemble as much information as possible on the first three elements of reality. They may even be asked to speculate on mysteries. But it is up to the policymaker to take the leap from what is knowable and plan for events that may be shrouded in mystery, for what is required at this point is essentially a political judgment.

THE INFLUENCE OF POLICY AND THE
LIMITS OF DISSENT

One other potential hazard for analysis lies in the connection between intelligence producers and intelligence consumers that can also lead to intelligence failures. Experience shows that policy itself can influence intelligence, and, in many respects, this factor—the link between the analyst and the policymaker—can be the most difficult factor in the analysis process to manage. However, it is important to understand how policy can shape intelligence because the effects are more subtle than they are commonly portrayed by the press. Occasionally one sees a story in the media reporting how an intelligence analyst was pressured to change his assessment to please a supervisor or to conform with policy. This sometimes happens, but such cases are probably quite rare simply because such pressure is usually unnecessary.

First, the ability of intelligence to change the basic course of national policy is probably exaggerated; certainly the impact of any single estimate is rather limited. Despite the fact that most theories of foreign policy decision making argue that a direct relationship exists between intelligence and foreign policy, this relationship is usually greatly overstated.[24] The memoirs of presidents Nixon and Carter and of their national security advisers, for example, are revealing. Though they cite numerous instances in which intelligence provided warning or factual information, they are strikingly silent on any specific role that intelligence analysis may have played in the development of foreign policy. This is to be expected; Nixon, Carter, Henry Kissinger, and Zbigniew Brzezinski all had firm ideas as to what they thought the goals of U.S. foreign policy should be, and they did not need an NIE to tell them this.

Moreover, a range of views usually exists in the intelligence community on most issues. So, if an official does not agree with the assessment that one agency provides him, he is likely to be able to find one more supportive from some other agency. It is worth noting that in virtually every case that has been studied of an alleged intelligence failure between 1960 and 1980, the investigators have concluded that even if the intelligence community had possessed the right information or had reached the correct judgment, the policymakers would probably have ignored or rejected their findings. Indeed, one of the first things that an intelligence officer learns is that on most issues—and especially political and economic ones—the policymaker often functions as his own analyst.[25]

When policy biases intelligence it is less often because of pressure than because an analyst decides on his own not to press a case that seems too out of step with current thinking. The continual problems the U.S. intelligence community has had in diverging from conventional wisdom in its assessments concerning Iran are a case in point. The failure to predict the fall of the Shah and to anticipate the actions of the Khomeini regime could at least in part be traced to U.S. policy regarding Iran. The intelligence community in the early and mid-1970s concluded that the Shah was unlikely to be toppled; whether by coincidence or not, this assessment was consistent with U.S. policy, which was based on the premise that the Shah was secure. According to Brzezinski, the belief in the Shah was so ingrained that contrary information was dismissed out of hand, if it was obtained at all. It has been documented that U.S. efforts to maintain friendly relations with the Shah also resulted in a reluctance of the intelligence community to develop independent intelligence sources in Iran.[26]

The best defense against this kind of bias is to insist that estimates on which policy is being based be subjected to communitywide scrutiny. As we shall see in the next chapter, adding different points of view to the formulation of an estimate does not in itself necessarily guarantee better intelligence. But the prospects of exposing an incorrect assessment, and especially an incorrect assessment that is being promoted for policy reasons, improve with the number of critics who have access to it. Intelligence errors are more likely to persist when they are protected from criticism, as was illustrated in the Iran-Contra affair. Analysts throughout the intelligence community believed that the prospects of finding a "moderate" faction in the Iranian leadership were minimal, but the proponents of the policy insulated themselves from unfavorable intelligence assessments by resorting to extraordinary secrecy.[27] The ill-advised initiative might have proceeded even if contrary analysis had been aired, but cutting out dissenters virtually insured that policy was never subjected to a true sanity check.

In any case, one has to be realistic about the power of intelligence. Past experience suggests that intelligence information and judgments are ill-equipped for settling contentious disputes over policy. For the most part, the general direction of policy is almost always settled by politics, and intelligence is most effective when it is used to assist those who implement that policy after it is selected. This may not be encouraging from the viewpoint of the intelligence specialist, but in a democracy we would not want it to be otherwise.

FIVE

Intelligence and Problems of Organization

Most studies of strategic intelligence analysis address problems such as those discussed in the previous chapter, namely the difficulty of interpreting data, modeling events that cannot be observed directly, or detecting warning signals amidst the noise of day-to-day events. These studies all share a common trait: they tend to describe the process of analysis from the perspective of an individual analyst and emphasize the difficulties associated with their interpretation of events. This perspective is adequate for analyzing many problems in intelligence. A mistake in analyzing a particular piece of evidence, for example, changes little if stated as "the CIA misinterpreted" rather than "an analyst misinterpreted," or as "State's Bureau of Intelligence and Research could not decipher" rather than "an analyst could not decipher."

Yet, as we shall see in this chapter, in addition to the problems inherent in collecting and analyzing data, intelligence errors can also be the result of malfunctions of intelligence organizations themselves—as in the case, for example, when an agency "loses" or delays transmission of a piece of information during processing, or when an interagency committee makes an incorrect choice in deciding which view to adopt in an intelligence assessment.

In truth, most intelligence estimates for major issues today are not produced by a single analyst. Rather, they are group efforts in which several analysts participate, often from different agencies within the intelligence community. In writing NIEs today, for example, the Chairman of the National Intelligence Council assigns one agency responsibility for preparing an initial draft (the NIC's Analytic Group, a small staff established in the early 1980s, also sometimes prepares drafts).

This draft is then circulated among the other agencies for comments, additions, and revisions.

Each agency is recognized as having expertise in a given field, sometimes formally, sometimes informally, and will usually be given responsibility for drafting estimates on that subject. So the CIA usually prepares most estimates on economic affairs, components within the Army Intelligence Agency usually take the lead in analyses of Soviet ground-to-air missiles, and so on. Overall, CIA officers draft about half of all NIEs.[1]

In other situations, the DCI may assemble an ad hoc team bringing together representatives from several agencies to follow a particular issue. This practice has been used more and more in recent years. For example, special analytical teams were established to monitor events during the Iranian Revolution and following the Soviet invasion of Afghanistan. An interagency team was also used during the late 1970s to analyze the Soviet civil defense system and the likelihood of another Arab-Israeli war. Either way, when analysis is done by organizations rather than individuals, new complications for intelligence are introduced.

THE PROBLEM OF DISSEMINATION OF DATA

The organization of the analysis components of the intelligence community reflect many of the beliefs of individuals such as William Langer and Sherman Kent, who were largely responsible for their development. The first of these beliefs was that the cataloguing and distribution of intelligence data should be controlled by a single, central office, and that all participants in drafting an estimate should have equal access to these data.

To Langer, Kent, and their colleagues, this principle was a lesson of the failure of U.S. intelligence to anticipate the surprise attack on Pearl Harbor and is the most frequently cited rationale for the establishment of the Central Intelligence Agency. The key word was not *agency* but *central*. Centralization was intended to minimize the chances that warning signals would be overlooked or lost in the noise of routine events or in a bureaucratic snafu. In addition to the "signal-to-noise" problem, the Pearl Harbor failure lay in distribution of the information. The circulation of the MAGIC intercepts was extremely limited. According to official records, the distribution list for MAGIC in Washington included just nine officials. Because MAGIC was so restricted, no one was able to see the overall pattern that would have revealed Japanese preparations.[2]

But the Pearl Harbor failure really pointed out a broader problem in the U.S. intelligence apparatus. It was not just that the right data did not get to the right offices in this particular case; no one in the intelligence community had a vantage point from which to understand the broader importance of a piece of information so that its distribution could be decided intelligently. In 1941, the agencies that collected intelligence disseminated it as they saw fit. The Office of Naval Intelligence collected MAGIC, so it decided who would be on the distribution list. Unfortunately, ONI officials understood MAGIC only in the context of their own work, and so they were simply in no position to understand how MAGIC might be critical to another agency, or to a national estimate.

Indeed, not only was MAGIC distributed ineffectively; there was even some confusion as to whom was receiving the intelligence. Admiral Stark, Chief of Naval Operations, for example, thought the commander of naval forces at Pearl Harbor, Admiral Kimmel, received MAGIC, when in fact he had been taken off the distribution list four months earlier. Similarly, the Army's intelligence staff in Washington, erroneously believing that the Navy's intelligence staff at Pearl Harbor was passing MAGIC to General Short, the Army commander in Hawaii, did not pass him this intelligence through its own channels.[3]

Although opponents of a peacetime OSS were temporarily able to kill a central agency for intelligence analysis, they could not counter the argument for keeping a single official in charge of organizing and disseminating raw intelligence data. So, when the OSS was dissolved in the months following

World War II, President Truman retained a National Intelligence Authority and a Central Intelligence Group to ensure the proper dissemination of data and routing of intelligence to the appropriate consumers. The National Intelligence Authority evolved into the office of the Director of Central Intelligence, and, later, when the DCI was given a statutory basis under the National Security Act of 1947, his formal responsibilities included "to correlate and evaluate intelligence relating to the national security, and provide for the appropriate dissemination of such intelligence within the Government using where appropriate existing agencies and facilities."[4]

This language gives the DCI formal authority over the dissemination of intelligence, but the qualification "formal" is important. In practice, the heads of the agencies responsible for collection still have considerable say. In addition to increasing the DCI's control over the tasking and development of intelligence systems, Stansfield Turner tried, without much success, to reform the guidelines used to classify sensitive intelligence during his tenure as DCI. In theory, access to Special Compartmented Intelligence (SCI) information is decided by the DCI, but in practice, it is usually negotiated between the managers of the collection program and the office of the analyst seeking access.

At the time Turner was DCI, about fifty codewords were in use within the intelligence community. Turner believed that this system was complicated, cumbersome, and ineffective. He thought that a system consisting of fifty different compartments was both difficult to enforce and inefficient. Turner proposed to consolidate the fifty-odd codewords into a system of just five. He was opposed by program managers at NSA and other agencies who, naturally, were inclined to defend their organizational turf and feared that intelligence sources for which they were responsible would be compromised. These program managers stalled in implementing Turner's directive, so that by 1981 Turner had left office and the agencies continued to control their own codewords.[5]

If a problem of access to intelligence data exists today, it is more subtle than that which existed prior to Pearl Harbor.

Today, with a few exceptions, at least the heads of all agencies responsible for analysis have access to most intelligence data. It is also unlikely that any National Intelligence Officer is denied access to information relevant to his function.

The difficulty occurs at the lower levels of the organization: the line analysts, who actually develop the institutional opinion of their agency on intelligence issues, sometimes lack access to sensitive information that might alter some of their conclusions. The decision to grant access to these individuals is usually settled far below the level of the DCI—indeed, usually such decisions are made according to standard operating procedures. As a result, making sure that classification does not hinder the typical analyst is a catch-as-catch-can problem that depends on how well middle-level managers detect such problems and are able to appeal the case to the powers that be.

Furthermore, even after an analyst acquires access, he is sometimes prevented from citing the data in his product. On other occasions the analyst may only be able to cite a "sensitive source." Intelligence reports rarely indicate the precise origin of the data being used, but, at a minimum, it is usually clear in generic terms from where the data originated. So, for example, the reader may not know precisely which collection system was used to obtain a datum—usually even the analyst will not know that—but he will usually understand whether the information is from, say, telemetry, doctrinal literature, or casual conversations in the diplomatic circuit. This helps the reader decide how much confidence to place in the report and to put the report into context.

With especially perishable sources, such as human agents who could be identified on the basis of the information they provide, the citation may simply be a "sensitive source." The result, unfortunately, is often similar to that of a newspaper article that refers to "anonymous sources." The reliability of the story is brought into question or is thought to be distorted. The reader may thus mistake truly critical information from a valuable source as just another piece of information, or, alternatively, the reader might exaggerate the information's importance.

A second key problem today is access by analysts to classified, *non-intelligence* data. Though the DCI is responsible for classifying intelligence material, other officials are responsible for protecting U.S. diplomatic or military information. For example, the Under Secretary of Defense for Policy is responsible for classification of U.S. military secrets. As a result, the DCI cannot authorize an intelligence analyst to be given information pertaining to a "black" (or "SAR," for "special access required") weapon program.

Accordingly, intelligence analysts will sometimes lack information that might otherwise alter their assessments. For example, prior to 1980, when the Carter administration announced the development of the Advanced Technology Bomber as a replacement to the B-1, no U.S. official made any public reference to the development by the United States of low-observable "stealth" aircraft technology—even though such technology was being developed by the Defense Department for at least fifteen years.[6] Most intelligence analysts responsible for assessing aerospace systems were probably aware of the principles of limiting radar cross-sections, but many, if not most, were unaware of U.S. efforts in the field.

If the Soviets had learned of U.S. efforts in this field and had taken actions in response—say, if the Soviets invested in bistatic radar, facilities for measuring radar cross-sections, and other systems associated with efforts to defeat stealth technology—American intelligence analysts unfamiliar with stealth would probably be at a loss to explain these actions. A similar error might occur if the Soviets took diplomatic steps to counter stealth—such as proposing limitations on stealthy systems in arms control negotiations—and U.S. analysts attempting to explain the Soviet negotiating position lacked knowledge of the American program the Soviets were actually trying to curb.

Analytic gaps and errors can also occur when intelligence officials lack knowledge of U.S. diplomatic or military plans, which are also usually classified separately from the channels used to protect intelligence sources and methods. For instance, military officials rarely share the specific details of military contingency plans with civilians. As a result, U.S. analysts, lacking an understanding of, say, U.S. logistical planning for the reinforcement of NATO, might not understand or might not be alert to the Soviet development of operational maneuver groups that the Soviets intend to use to disrupt these reinforcement operations.

Similarly, knowledge of U.S. military or diplomatic plans might provide U.S. analysts with a better appreciation of foreign plans. During the 1950s and 1960s, for example, many civilian intelligence analysts believed that the Soviets would not use their intermediate-range bombers against the United States because they lacked the range for a round-trip flight. These analysts might have had a different view if they knew that some U.S. plans at the time called for our own intermediate-range bombers to make such one-way missions.

The problem is probably most pronounced, though, when U.S. intelligence is cut out of the loop of direct dealings senior American officials have with foreign governments. When this happens, not only do analysts lack information they need to provide accurate assessment, they are not even in a position to know what the intelligence requirements of the officials really are.

Resolving this problem requires a tradeoff between security and efficiency, and, as usual, there is probably no neat solution. Any classification system imposed to protect information is bound to cause some loss in the effectiveness of that information. Also, the problem should not be overstated. An intelligence failure the magnitude of Pearl Harbor is unlikely to result simply from overcompartmentation today. Access to information is now much more widespread than when the modern intelligence community was first established. Just to cite one example, in 1944—the height of World War II—just fifty thousand men and women had access to high-level SIGINT, while today the number of personnel with comparable access is approximately ten times as many.[7] And "informal access" (another name for circumventing compartmentation) also inevitably occurs. A CIA or DIA analyst responsible for analyzing the Soviet threat to the Persian Gulf is, as often as not, a former Army officer who was assigned to the Rapid Deployment Force, had access to U.S. military planning for the region, and knows how to get an unofficial update.

The most critical costs imposed by compartmentation appear to lie in two areas. First, security impedes creative analysis. Limiting the number of analysts who have access to a channel of data inherently limits the likelihood that some analyst somewhere in the intelligence community will think of a new way to use the information. Second, security reduces the responsiveness of the community to its consumers because it limits the people who are able to work on a project or because of delays in the circulation of necessary information.

PROBLEMS OF COORDINATING INTELLIGENCE IN ORGANIZATIONS

Even assuming that information is disseminated among analysts with maximum efficiency and perfect security, another set of organizational problems can arise once these analysts interpret the data. The difficulty lies in reconciling the views of different parties whenever more than one agency—or, for that matter, more than one analyst—participates in drafting an intelligence estimate. This reconciliation usually takes the form of coordination, in which a draft estimate is circulated for review, modification, and eventually approval by the member agencies within the intelligence community.

Coordination is a process of deciding which views will be included in the estimate and which, if any, will be left out or labeled as dissents. In principle, coordination is supposed to result in a better intelligence product. If coordination works as hoped, it will identify the more accurate conclusions and eliminate the less accurate ones. During the early years of the intelligence community, intelligence experts assumed that coordination did indeed accomplish these objectives and hence improved estimates. Unfortunately, as will be seen, this is often not true. Coordination cannot only fail to work as promised but it can also present its own opportunities for producing error or making an estimate unresponsive to the needs of the intelligence consumer.

Consequently, Langer and Kent believed that national estimates should be drafted by a relatively small group of experts. They believed that this staff should be kept separate from the other agencies but that it should base its draft estimates on the analysis already existing within the community rather than on its own basic research.

In the plan presented in *Strategic Intelligence*, Sherman Kent would have made the CIA itself this staff. He proposed that the Director of Central Intelligence should be in charge of national estimates and that the CIA should be an integrator of intelligence rather than a producer. Kent envisioned the analytical components of the CIA as being a limited body of "intelligence renaissance men": analysts who would keep up with the latest intelligence produced by the State Department and the armed services and who would synthesize these findings to formulate a draft of the national estimate. This draft would be circulated through the intelligence community for comment, modified, and finally delivered by the DCI and his board of advisors to the President.[8]

The CIA could have performed this function under the provisions of the National Security Act of 1947, and the CIG included a Central Reports Staff, which was intended to correlate community intelligence.[9] Yet, even as Kent was writing in 1948 and 1949, the CIA was developing in a way that made the agency itself a producer of "departmental intelligence." As a result, another organization would have to be created to fulfill Kent's vision.

One reason the CIA became an intelligence producer, rather than simply a coordinator and disseminator of intelligence, was that the military services were unwilling to work with the CIA on estimates. For example, CIA analysts initially were not allowed access to intelligence that contained certain categories of data collected by the military, such as SIGINT.

As Anthony Downs, an economist who has studied organizational behavior, has observed, bureaucracies tend to adapt in order to survive. If the demand for the original mission of an organization disappears, the individuals within it will try to establish new missions for the organization, hoping to attract a market for these services. Hence, when CIA officials found that they could not distribute the intelligence of other agencies, they used what production capability they had on hand to produce their own product, at the time called the *Daily*, and found a potential audience—the President. They then fine-tuned their product to his needs, thus ensuring their organization's continued survival. However, by responding to these incentives and concentrating on the current reporting that comprised the *Daily*, rather than coordinating intelligence, the CIA was diverted from the mission for which it was originally intended.[10]

So, by 1950, the CIA had already developed its own component for independent analysis, the Office of Research and Evaluation (ORE). As one might expect from the example of other bureaucracies, once established, ORE was unlikely to be eliminated. Forming the core of several offices that specialized in current intelligence, scientific intelligence, library support, and so on, ORE was the basis of what later became the Directorate of Intelligence.

A second factor contributing to the development of the CIA's offices for independent analysis was the emergence of intelligence topics that fell between the cracks of the responsibilities of the State Department and the Defense Department. These topics, which were to prove increasingly important, included economic analysis and scientific intelligence and, in particular, basic science, health sciences, and space science. State Department personnel tended to concentrate on traditional political affairs rather than the relatively newer field of international finance. The military services tended to ignore science and technology that did not have a direct military application. The CIA's charter allowed it to cover subjects that were not covered by the existing intelligence agencies, and it responded by establishing the Office of Scientific Intelligence (OSI) and the Office of Research and Reports (ORR). Thus, by 1950, the CIA already possessed a considerable analytical team of its own, numbering between six hundred and nine hundred persons.[11]

Kent's recommended small staff for developing national estimates was realized later, when Walter Bedell Smith invited Langer to reform the national estimate production process. Langer then established the Board of National Estimates and its supporting staff, the Office of National Estimates. These organizations met Kent's prescription almost to the letter: the BNE was composed of "men of stature" (former diplomats, combat commanders, and academics, all with outstanding credentials), while ONE consisted of selected analysts who were judged especially qualified for the "correlation and synthesis" duties of the office. Also, the staff was small. Legend has it that Smith offered Langer two hundred personnel slots, only for Langer to reply that he could make do with twenty-five.[12]

However, ONE departed from Kent's guidelines in at least one important aspect: the analysts selected for ONE were mainly drawn from the analytic organs that had developed within the CIA rather than from the community as a whole. One reason for this was that Langer and, later, Kent handpicked their staff. They naturally tended to select individuals whose work they had come to respect from personal experience, and these happened to be mainly CIA personnel. Another reason was that a posting to ONE was not helpful to the career of either a military intelligence officer or a Foreign Service officer, especially in the early days when the State Department and the military services were resisting the development of the CIA and the institutions associated with the NIE. As a result, intentional or not, ONE drafts generally tended to reflect CIA views.

The procedures for coordinating national estimates reflected some of the attitudes common to early twentieth-century historians such as Langer and Kent. They assumed that criticism improves analysis and that competition among different analysts yields more accurate predictions. The idea was that a "best truth" would emerge when the coordination process was over. Coordination also reflected political realities. It would have been impossible for the Director of Central Intelligence to represent an NIE as the best thinking within the intelligence community unless Defense and State were able to have some say over what went into the estimate. The process of coordinating estimates enabled the DCI to accommodate the views of community members where necessary and also allowed the DCI to generate support for the NIE from community members by allowing them to identify the specific points upon which they had significant disagreements.

The formal process of writing a National Intelligence Estimate would thus proceed as follows.

One member of the BNE would be appointed chairman of the estimate. Usually this board member was an individual with special expertise in the topic addressed by the estimate, such as, for instance, the NIE on Soviet strategic forces was usually chaired by a former military officer. The chairman of the estimate would, with the approval of the rest of the board, draft the "terms of reference" for the estimate, an outline of the issues that the estimate was supposed to address.

These terms of reference were then circulated among agencies within the intelligence community. The participants in any single estimate varied over time, but usually they included the agencies represented on the community's "board of directors"—originally the Intelligence Advisory Committee (IAC), later the U.S. Intelligence Board (USIB), currently the National Foreign Intelligence Board (NFIB). In each of its incarnations, this group included the heads of the principal members of the community. Its membership varied as agencies were created or consolidated. For example, the original IAC was chaired by the DCI and included representatives from the Department of State, Army, Air Force, Joint Chiefs of Staff, and the Atomic Energy Commission. When the DIA was created in 1961, it supplanted the heads of the military intelligence services on what had by then become USIB. Similarly, the AEC was replaced by the Department of Energy in 1977 in NFIB.

After the terms of reference were approved, the ONE staff

wrote a draft version of the estimate, which was circulated within the community. This draft was intended to reflect the community's current understanding of the subject. The draft also became the starting point for discussions and negotiations over the language of the estimate. Each recipient of the draft would prepare a response, recommending changes where it saw fit.

The sections of the NIE were then coordinated informally at the staff level, analyst-to-analyst, and, later, in a formal session in which representatives from each agency went paragraph by paragraph through the estimate. At this point, a representative could indicate where his agency would want to dissent from the text of the estimate in a footnote. The resulting draft of the estimate, with dissents, would then be presented to the BNE for its review.

The final version of NIEs were presented to USIB (later NFIB) and the DCI for approval. Although modifications could still be made at this point, this review was mainly *pro forma* and intended to put the views of the community members on record. The arguments and counterarguments would have been heard before, and, in most cases, the principals had already taken an active part in the estimate behind the scenes by working through their staffs.

Most NIEs continue to follow this general process, though much depends on how urgently the estimate is needed. Regularly produced NIEs, such as estimates on Soviet military forces, require about a year to turn out. Other estimates require just a few months. Special National Intelligence Estimates (SNIEs), intended to reflect the community's views in a fast-breaking situation, can be produced in a matter of days.

THE EVOLUTION OF NIEs AND THEIR USE

Though the essential procedure for producing NIEs has remained more or less the same over the years, many specific details have varied, reflecting changes in the intelligence bureaucracy and the importance different administrations have assigned to NIEs.

During the 1950s and early 1960s, for example, NIEs had considerable influence in the higher strata of the executive branch. Their influence declined somewhat in the later 1960s, and even more during the Nixon administration. One reason was that, largely at the behest of Henry Kissinger, NIEs were greatly enlarged to present more data for the reader to use in drawing his own conclusions. They were also written to present judgments in a more qualified and substantiated fashion, unlike the earlier approach, which was allegedly characterized by Kissinger as "talmudic." Also, whereas in early years the NIE was usually the only official document presenting a systematic, community-coordinated assessment of an intelligence topic, the NIE today has considerable competition.

For example, in addition to NIEs, the DCI today issues a number of other types of intelligence reports. One of these is the Interagency Intelligence Memorandum (IIM), which is produced and coordinated much in the same way as NIEs but which is not submitted to the NFIB for approval. Interagency Intelligence Memoranda also tend to focus on narrower topics than do NIEs. Recent examples of IIMs include the community studies on Soviet civil defense measures in the late 1970s and early 1980s.

During the 1980s, the Reagan administration decided that the intelligence community should refocus its efforts on NIEs. One result was that the number of NIEs produced by the community each year approximately tripled, from an average of twelve produced in the late 1970s to as many as thirty-eight in one recent year.[13] Even so, it is unlikely that the NIE will regain the role it played in the 1950s and early 1960s in supporting the development of key policies, if only because today individual agencies within the community often issue their own comprehensive, all-source intelligence. These reports can be just as voluminous and professionally turned out as NIEs. Interestingly, the coordination process within the agencies resembles the interagency coordination of NIEs and IIMs. The various offices within each agency tend to develop their own institutional points of view, which they defend vigorously.

Since the early 1970s, for example, the Department of Defense has issued its own coordinated intelligence under the auspices of the Director of the Defense Intelligence Agency. These "Defense Intelligence Estimates" (DIEs) are used within the Department of Defense for planning and were created in accord with the DIA's assignment to provide intelligence support to the Secretary of Defense, the Joint Chiefs of Staff, and other Defense Department components.

These DIEs, together with other Defense Department products, such as Defense Estimative Briefs (DEBs), System Threat Assessment Reports (STARs), and various data bases maintained under the General Defense Intelligence Program, are coordinated among Defense Department intelligence agencies but not other members of the community, such as the CIA, the Department of Energy, or INR. These DoD intelligence publications are important because, under current regulations, they can be used instead of community-coordinated NIEs in Defense Department and National Security Council planning. For example, DoD agencies produce the intelligence used in developing military contingency plans.[14] Similarly, the intelligence used in the development of U.S. weapon systems is almost always a DoD product.

Under the provisions of most regulations granting the Director of DIA authority to coordinate intelligence among Defense Department agencies, he is technically supposed to ensure that these estimates conform with nationally coordinated intelligence. In practice, though, the agencies often have considerable latitude, as in the case when, for example, "intelligence support" consists of the day-to-day relationship between a DIA or an Army Intelligence analyst and a staff member of U.S. Central Command preparing contingency plans for operations in the Middle East.

Even interagency committees within the IC Staff occasionally issue products that can be considered intelligence assessments. For example, the IC Staff committees responsible for planning collection systems require assessments of likely intelligence targets in order to establish the specifications of the system. These assessments, which often amount to intelligence estimates and are issued under the DCI's own logo, appear as part of IC Staff planning studies. Since they are directly connected to policy decisions (that is, the planning document itself), these assessments fill the role of a formal intelligence estimate.

THE RECORD OF NIES AND THE ORGANIZATIONAL SOURCES OF ERROR

The record of NIEs for accuracy during the past several decades has been mixed, as one would expect of any set of intelligence forecasts. For example, figures 5.1 through 5.4 illustrate the record of NIEs in making two-, three-, and four-year forecasts of Soviet ICBM deployments between 1957, when the Soviets tested their first ICBM, the SS-6, and 1972, when SALT I capped ICBM launchers. The ranges are the Soviet deployments the NIE forecasted for a particular year. The trend line indicates the number of ICBMs the Soviets actually deployed. So, for instance, figure 5.4 indicates that in 1963 the NIE predicted that four years later in 1967 the Soviets would have 300 to 525 ICBMs operational, while the actual number was 570. As can be seen, the community tended to overestimate Soviet deployments in the late 1950s, provided fairly accurate estimates in the early 1960s, and considerably underestimated Soviet ICBM deployments in the mid- and late-1960s.

These errors had a number of causes, ranging from a simple lack of information to problems of method. There has also been another source of error in national estimates, however: the procedure through which estimates have been coordinated within the intelligence community.

The Problem of Coordination

As mentioned earlier, coordination is intended to improve estimates. Specifically, one would hope that coordination would bring more wisdom to bear on a problem and that, if a mem-

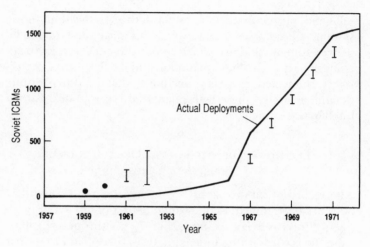

FIGURE 5.1
Two-Year Forecasts of Soviet ICBMs

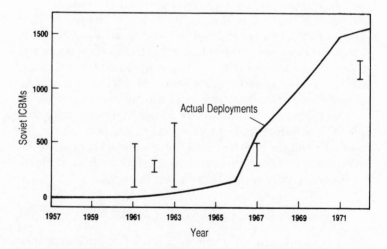

FIGURE 5.2
Three-Year Forecasts of Soviet ICBMs

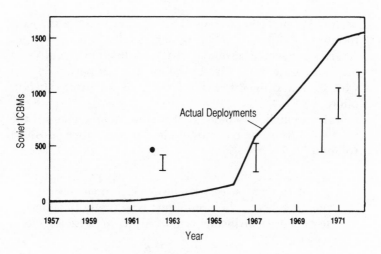

FIGURE 5.3
Four-Year Forecasts of Soviet ICBMs

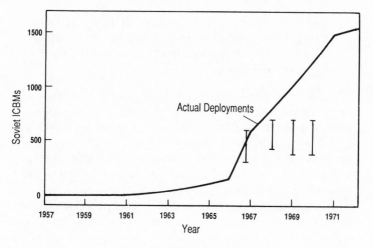

FIGURE 5.4
Five-Year Forecasts of Soviet ICBMs

ber of the intelligence community has an accurate forecast, the process of coordination would identify it as such. Conversely, one would also hope that coordination would weed out inaccurate forecasts. Certainly these expectations are what Kent and the other founders of the NIE process had in mind.

Unfortunately, although coordination might identify the best estimate in the community, it also opens three possible routes to failure:[15]

— The community, considering all viewpoints on an equal footing, selects an incorrect estimate because one member of the community is wrong but happens to be more convincing or more astute in presenting its views.

— The community begins with the assumption that one member has greater expertise in a field, or that a particular point of view is more plausible than others. This assumption, if valid, will keep the final estimate from going too far astray, but if it is invalid, the estimate will be biased toward an inaccurate conclusion.

— The community simply accepts all views as having equal validity, making the estimate the "least common denominator" of wisdom in the community and leaving divisive issues unresolved.

The errors stemming from coordination become clear when one considers the forecasts of Soviet ICBM deployments published in the intelligence community's NIE on Soviet strategic forces from the late 1950s to the early 1970s. These forecasts have received much attention over the years, in part because of their political impact. What is often overlooked, however, is that these errors were at least as much a problem of coordinating intelligence as they were a problem of analysis. In almost every case, at least one agency did in fact arrive at the correct forecast, only to see its estimate rejected or modified to accommodate other members of the community. In the case of the underestimates of Soviet ICBM deployments in NIEs of the late 1950s and early 1960s, the Army and the Navy appear to have arrived at the correct estimate but lost out in coordination. At the time these estimates were drafted, the Soviet Union had just tested its first-generation ICBM, the ss-6, and the intelligence community attempted to predict how rapidly the Soviets would develop an operational ICBM force. The community lacked much hard evidence in those days. The only imagery that was available, for example, was from U-2 overflights, and this coverage was sporadic and incomplete.[16]

As a result, the participants on the NIE on Soviet strategic weapons had a range of views. All of these views had at least some support from the available data: the Air Force predicted the Soviets would initiate an all-out production effort in order to counter U.S. superiority in manned bombers; the Army and Navy argued that the Soviets would opt for a minimal deployment of ss-6s, waiting to begin full-scale ICBM production with the more effective second-generation ss-7 and ss-8; the CIA believed that the Soviets would deploy some ss-6s to offset the U.S. advantage in strategic weapons, but, because of the potential advantage promised by the later systems, not in the numbers predicted by the Air Force.

As it happened, the CIA view held sway, in part because it had the favorable status of being the "median view," and in part because the CIA had a dominant position in coordinating national estimates at that time. This estimate, it turned out, was incorrect, leading to the famous "missile gap" controversy of the 1960 presidential election. The Army and Navy analysts were proven right, and even the CIA's middle position overestimated eventual Soviet deployments.[17]

(In truth, the CIA's estimate was itself a compromise. The analysts in ONE had arrived at estimates for Soviet ICBM deployments that were about the same as those of the Army. However, their supervisors disagreed, believing that Soviet deployments would be somewhat higher. In speaking with analysts who took part in this estimate, it appears that the final position taken by the CIA was shaded toward the supervisors' higher estimate.)

The following decade, the coordination process again filtered out more correct estimates in favor of less correct ones but with the opposite effect. Instead of overestimates, the process was partly responsible for a series of underestimates. Again, several views were argued in the intelligence community: the Air Force, as before, had the highest estimate but was joined this time by the other military services; the State Department's INR had the lowest estimate; the CIA once again had the median position. The Air Force argued that the Soviets would build new ICBMs to the maximum capacity allowed by their production facilities and would not dismantle their old missiles. The rationale of INR was that the Soviets would deploy only a "minimal deterrent" and would not seek parity with the United States. The CIA again had a position in between the two extremes.

In this case, the community's final coordinated estimate amounted to the range between the lowest Air Force estimate and the point estimated by INR. Alas, this estimate proved too low, and the NIE underestimated Soviet ICBM deployments during most of the 1960s, when Soviet ICBM deployments eventually surpassed those of the United States. In retrospect, it appears that, had the community adopted the Air Force's highest estimates, it would have been correct.[18]

Thus, in both cases, at least some analysts in the community correctly forecast Soviet ICBM deployments, but their views were kept out of the NIE or relegated to footnotes by the process of coordination. Also, both sets of errors had significant repercussions. The early underestimates led John Kennedy to commit himself to a strategic arms program that he was compelled to carry out once in office, even though the threat on which it was grounded proved to be exaggerated. The later underestimates of the 1960s undermined the credibility of the intelligence community and contributed to its political problems in the 1970s.[19]

In retrospect, it is easy to criticize and to postulate that the Missile Gap affair would not have occurred if the NIE in 1959 had been left to the Army, or that the estimates of the 1960s would have been accurate had the national estimate just been left to Air Force analysts. Yet this criticism ignores the real choices intelligence officials had at the time. The officials responsible for the NIE could have acceded to the Army in the late 1950s or to the Air Force in the 1960s, but this would have amounted to biasing the estimate before it was drafted, and it is only in retrospect that we know what the best bias would have been. After all, it is precisely because we did *not* know what the future Soviet ICBM deployments would be that an NIE was needed. Alternatively, the officials could have just presented three separate, uncoordinated estimates, or a single estimate incorporating all views. In either case, no information would have been added. Indeed, this would have obscured the different rationales that led to the various estimates.

The Role of Competitive Analysis in Organizations

The errors of the national estimate on Soviet strategic forces received considerable attention in the early 1970s, when Albert Wohlstetter publicized the underestimates that had been produced during the preceding decade.[20] News of the underestimates had circulated in classified channels during the first years of the Nixon administration. Secretary of Defense Melvin Laird, for example, reported what had occurred to the Senate and House Armed Services Committee in closed session. Wohlstetter managed to have portions of the classified annex of the Secretary of Defense's Posture Statements for 1962 to 1973 released. Each year the Secretary had presented projections drawn from the NIE for anticipated Soviet strategic force deployments, and this revealed the errors that had occurred. (The declassified annexes Wohlstetter obtained were the source of the estimates in the 1960s that appear in figures 5.1 through 5.4.)

Following this revelation, successive DCIs James Schlesinger and William Colby were pressed to take some response. It fell to George Bush, DCI after 1975, to commission the now-famous "B Team exercise." This exercise was designed to investigate whether the NIE could be improved by "competitive analysis." The method allowed two sets of analysts—an "A Team" and a "B Team"—to address the same problem. Each team was allowed to reach its own conclusions. The conclusions were then compared, and the participants attempted to reconcile their differences. This attempt at formal competitive analysis helped encourage modifications to the process of developing NIEs (although it must be pointed out that many of these changes had been in the process of being adopted since Schlesinger had been director). The most important modification was the approach taken to dissenting views in the NIE.*

Previously, dissenting agencies were allowed to indicate their dissents in a footnote to the main text of the NIE, giving their own view and a brief explanation of their rationale.

* The B Team exercise is often misrepresented in press accounts and even some scholarly works.

One distortion is simply that there was "a" single B Team. In truth, there were three B Teams: one on Soviet air defenses, one on Soviet missile accuracy, and one on Soviet intentions.

A second distortion is that the B Team exercise was itself responsible for a major change in U.S. estimates of Soviet military capabilities; in some of the more extreme distortions, the exercise is reported to have exposed CIA analysts who were supposedly "soft" in their views of the Soviet threat. In reality, the effects of the B Team exercise can better be characterized as "limited but useful." Certainly any impact the exercise had on the numbers appearing in various National Intelligence Estimates was indirect.

The analysts who took part in the B Team exercise examining Soviet air defenses and Soviet missile accuracy approached their issues by debating the subject until they understood the points of evidence on which they disagreed and then focusing their attention on those factors. By most accounts, intelligence on both Soviet air defense and Soviet missile accuracy was improved in the process and, as noted here, this is generally the approach that is taken on such estimates today.

The third B Team exercise, which addressed Soviet intentions, was, probably by the nature of the topic, less grounded in specific points of evidence. As a result, the B Team report merely posited a more hawkish view of Soviet preparations for war and the willingness of the Soviet Union to use force. This report had little impact on intelligence estimates or how the intelligence community conducts analysis today, but it has received almost all of the publicity concerning the B Team exercise.

Most public figures who cite a need for a "return" to competitive analysis ("another B Team") do not seem aware that, in fact, the benefits of such analysis are already included in coordinated intelligence products.

Needless to say, it was more difficult to develop an argument in a footnote than in the main text. Also, the implication of this format was that the main text was "the authoritative view" and should be given more credence than the footnote, which was apparently "the alternate view." In the new system, which was further developed when Turner was DCI, dissenters were required to elaborate their views in the main text and specify the precise basis for their disagreement. Footnotes were used primarily for identifying which members of the intelligence community subscribed to a given portion of the text.*

* Interestingly, in later years the opposite often happened; upon receiving a new NIE, readers would often skim through it to see where the footnotes appeared. One former official, for example, recalls looking for the "Keegangrams" in his copy of an NIE, referring to Major General George Keegan, the Air Force's Deputy Chief of Staff for Intelligence and a frequent dissenter from the community view. They knew that footnotes indicated which issues were more controversial. As a result, the footnoted sections of the NIEs—and possibly even the footnotes themselves—often received more attention than the rest of the estimate.

Of course, all of the participants took the coordination process most seriously, but the "game of the footnotes" sometimes produced results that are ironic in retrospect. One case is that of Major General Jack Thomas, one of Keegan's predecessors as head of Air Force intelligence.

Like Keegan, Thomas was a frequent dissenter in the community's NIEs on Soviet strategic forces, believing that the community view underestimated future Soviet deployments. One year the NFIB decided to include the name of the official requesting the footnote in the footnote itself. This was highly unusual, as the general practice is to identify the dissenter only by his institutional affiliation. So, where a footnote might usually read "the Assistant Chief of Staff for Intelligence, USAF, believes . . . ," the revised footnote read, "Maj. Gen. Jack Thomas, Assistant Chief of Staff for Intelligence, USAF, believes. . . ."

This change may have been intended to increase the costs of dissenting, as presumably one would be more reluctant to break from the intelligence community's consensus if the official requesting the dissent had to take personal responsibility. Air Force intelligence officers believed that civilian intelligence and defense officials did not appreciate their frequent dissents and wanted to discourage the practice (although these officials strongly deny this). In any case, the Air Force's forecasts for that year proved to be more accurate than those of the community consensus, and, as a result, Thomas has the rare distinction of being personally immortalized in a National Intelligence Estimate as the analyst who got the forecast right.

So, for example, before these changes were made a hypothetical NIE on the Soviet threat to Western Europe might read "the Soviet Army can mobilize its Category I and Category II divisions in 21 days," and a footnote might say that "the Director of the Defense Intelligence Agency believes that this view underestimates Soviet capabilities." Now an NIE will say "the majority view of the community is that Soviet Category I and II divisions can mobilize in 21 days, the main constraint being that tanks and other heavy equipment will require refurbishing before they can be used for battle," while the paragraph immediately following will say "another view holds that Soviet Category I and II divisions would require only 14 days to mobilize, as the Soviet Army is believed to have pre-positioned the components required for refurbishing." Each paragraph would be footnoted, so that the note for the first paragraph might indicate "the holders of this view are the Director for Intelligence, Central Intelligence Agency; the Director of Intelligence and Research, Department of State; and the Assistant Chief of Staff for Intelligence, U.S. Air Force," while the note for the second paragraph might indicate "The holders of this view are the Director, Defense Intelligence Agency; and Director, G-2, U.S. Army."

This approach to identifying dissents is significant because it connects the NIE and the coordination process to the planning of collection requirements and the development of future estimates. The current approach puts more emphasis on focusing the attention of intelligence analysts on specific questions that are, at least in principle, resolvable—questions such as, "How quickly do the hydraulic lines in Soviet tanks rot, and do the Soviets have adequate replacements stored in the garages housing the tanks for their Category II divisions?" Answering this question implies a requirement for certain specific information and, even if the necessary information cannot be obtained, at least the reader of the NIE has a precise understanding of what kinds of factors are responsible for the uncertainty. In other words, coordination has become the organizational equivalent of the process described in the preceding chapter through which an analyst reduces uncertainty.

A similar approach has been taken in recent years to deal with disagreement and uncertainty in predicting future events such as future Soviet military force development. In NIEs written in the early 1960s, the community would present, for example, a range for future Soviet ICBM deployments. This range had the appearance of a confidence interval developed with a given level of probability, and many readers appear to have interpreted these ranges in this way. In reality, such ranges represented a range of opinion that was accepted by consensus, by compromise, or sometimes simply by adding all of the estimates of the participating members of the intelligence community.

Today, NIEs projecting future Soviet deployments present several different scenarios, each based on a different set of assumptions. For example, a CIA analyst might believe that the Soviets will improve existing production facilities to accelerate their production of tanks, while a DIA analyst might believe that the Soviets will build new facilities for the same goal. The first estimate would show a faster rate of acceleration peaking at a lower level, while the second estimate would suggest a slower rate of acceleration in tank production that would eventually peak at a higher level. The disagreement between the two agencies might be based on different assessments concerning the Soviets' willingness to divert investment from civilian or other military production facilities. In today's NIEs, such a disagreement would be made clear and a projection for tank production plotted out for each scenario. This emphasis on explaining *why* analysts within the community disagree and identifying the factors responsible for these differences is in part a byproduct of the fact that today's NIEs are longer. This length allows each agency to explain its position in greater detail, sometimes in several paragraphs taking up the better part of a printed page.

It is always more satisfying to receive a simple, neat answer to a question such as how many tanks the Soviets will deploy next year, and a variety of projections, each based on a different set of assumptions, is inherently more difficult to comprehend. However, simply making clear *where* members of the community disagree and why may be the best we can do. It is not a perfect solution—it does not necessarily produce better intelligence in the short run and really only raises the problem of "coordination" from the level of the intelligence analyst to the level of the intelligence consumer. However, it is precisely in these cases, where intelligence cannot provide any additional basis for a decision, that elected or appointed officials *should* step in.

Yet, at least one other issue must be addressed before leaving the organizational problems of intelligence.

Though the errors of the intelligence community in forecasting Soviet missile deployments are cited in almost every current study of intelligence, one question that is rarely asked is, "Why did it take so long for the errors contained in the NIE on Soviet strategic forces to become apparent?" After all, the case of the underestimates of Soviet ICBMs occurred regularly over a period of almost ten years.

In a conversation with one of the authors, a former DCI said that he was not aware of this pattern until he had read the Wohlstetter articles in *Foreign Policy*—an unclassified assessment by a scholar who, though experienced in intelligence and defense affairs, was in fact an outsider to the intelligence community at the time. In looking back, said the former DCI, it seems simply that no one connected with the NIE raised the issue. Yet the underestimates were almost certainly noticed by many of the people who relied on the NIE in their daily work, such as Air Force target planners and DoD acquisition officials. These people almost certainly must have noticed that the NIE forecasts had become unreliable. Unfortunately, they do not appear to have been tied back into the NIE planning process. The lesson is that the problem of getting the product to the consumer and making certain that the consumer's needs have been met may be the most critical and most difficult challenge of all.

SIX

Some Immediate Issues: Funding, Personnel, Organization

In their discussions with the authors, one of the most interesting observations intelligence officials repeatedly made is that many of the problems that occupy their attention are not the intelligence problems that receive the most publicity. Possible moles in the higher levels of the CIA, the latest suspected Soviet arms control violation, and other high-profile issues are all important, of course. But the typical intelligence official usually is at least as concerned with the nuts-and-bolts issues of running a large organization faced with growing demands, rising costs, increasingly difficult missions, and a limited budget.

Three such issues, which we discuss in this chapter, will be especially important in the immediate future:

— how to ensure the intelligence community has the resources—that is, the funding—necessary to carry out the tasks most U.S. officials expect of it;

— how to ensure that the community will have the personnel necessary to carry out its missions; and

— how to ensure that the intelligence bureaucracy will be capable of responding to routine current demands while also remaining innovative enough to meet the changing intelligence demands of the future and the unexpected.

FUNDING

In the next few years, the intelligence community will have to face the double problem of having to pay for systems that are becoming more expensive, even while the intelligence budget remains approximately the same—or smaller.

The Intelligence Budget Process

The U.S. intelligence budget is almost entirely invisible, but it follows approximately the same review process as other items in the federal budget. The few departures from normal accounting and oversight procedures are mainly for the sake of security.

Intelligence operations are divided into two large programs in the U.S. government: the NFIP (National Foreign Intelligence Program) and TIARA (Tactical Intelligence and Related Activities), each accounting for about half of the total money spent by the United States on intelligence. The NFIP, as its name implies, includes mainly "national" intelligence, or intelligence that serves a nationwide constituency. NFIP programs include most of what fits the rubric of "strategic intelligence": analytic organizations such as the CIA's Directorate of Intelligence, DIA, and INR, and most large-scale collection operations such as NSA, the national space reconnaissance program, and the CIA's Directorate of Operations. The NFIP is managed by the Director of Central Intelligence.

The other half of U.S. intelligence spending, TIARA, mainly supports the military's tactical intelligence systems. Examples of TIARA programs include the early-warning Pave Paws radar systems that would be used to detect a missile attack against the United States and reconnaissance camera pods attached to Air Force and Navy aircraft. TIARA is managed for the Secretary of Defense by the Assistant Secretary of Defense for Command, Control, Communications, and Intelligence (or, as it is usually called, "C³I").

In reality, the division between "national" and "tactical" systems is less clear-cut than an organizational table might lead one to believe. Imagery or SIGINT collected through an NFIP system can be distributed to operational units in the field to inform commanders about local battlefield conditions. Similarly, TIARA systems often have significant national-level applications. For example, the North American Aerospace Defense Command (NORAD) maintains a regularly updated database on objects orbiting the earth, ranging from satellites to spent missile boosters to a glove lost by a Gemini astronaut during a spacewalk in the 1960s. These operations are mainly supported by TIARA funds, but the information they produce is usually available to analysts in NFIP programs as well.

In either case, the budget process is essentially the same: the Office of Management and Budget (OMB) provides the administration's guidance for each program's budget request for the upcoming fiscal year to the Director of Central Intelligence (in the case of NFIP) and the Secretary of Defense (in the case of TIARA). Program managers in the intelligence community and the Department of Defense then "build" the NFIP and TIARA, and the resulting budget requests are reported back to OMB. Each January, the administration presents its proposed budget for the next fiscal year to Congress, and these budget requests are reviewed by the appropriate committees.

Most of this activity goes on unseen by the public because the intelligence budget is classified. At each step in the normal budget process, the executive branch and Congress take the intelligence budget out of the overall federal budget, decide intelligence spending issues, and then re-insert the resulting figures into the appropriate unclassified budget lines. (These budget lines are usually large enough to allow the hidden intelligence funding to go unnoticed.) The budget is then sent to the next stage of the budget process, where the procedure is repeated.

Defense Spending and Intelligence

The immediate problem is that the intelligence community will require more money to carry out the missions expected of it, while, simultaneously, a declining defense budget will increase pressure to cut intelligence spending.* Exact figures

* Although the declining defense budget will be responsible for the great-

for intelligence spending are classified, but traditionally intelligence spending has followed defense spending: fat years for defense have been fat years for intelligence, and lean years for defense have been lean years for intelligence. The main reason is that intelligence is tied to defense through the budget process.

One obvious link is that about half of all intelligence spending—the TIARA budget—is indeed defense spending. TIARA systems are budgeted along with other defense systems, and so TIARA programs must compete with other defense programs in the Defense Department's annual budget review. Hence, in a year when strategic bombers and aircraft carriers are feeling the pinch, TIARA programs such as phased array radars for tracking objects in space and engine upgrades for SR-71 aircraft are likely to feel the pinch, too.

But it is not just tactical intelligence that is tied to the defense budget; the NFIP is linked to defense, too, by virtue of the fact that most NFIP programs are hidden in the defense budget in order to keep them secret. There are exceptions—the budgets of the Intelligence Community Staff and the CIA Retirement Fund are unclassified, and some intelligence operations are contained in the budgets of the State, Energy, and Justice departments—but these are minuscule, being measured merely in millions of dollars, while the rest of the NFIP is measured in billions. Hiding the intelligence budget inside the defense budget has the side effect of linking decisions on intelligence spending levels to decisions concerning military spending levels. This linkage is especially insidious because it can result in reductions in intelligence funding even when government officials and public opinion generally

---

est dollar effect on intelligence capabilities, the effects of cuts in other national security budgets will also spill over into intelligence. Possibly the most critical problem is the series of severe cuts that have been imposed on the State Department budget. As mentioned earlier, about four-fifths of all HUMINT is taken from the reporting of overt Foreign Service officers—a fact usually neglected when imposing reductions in embassy staffs and closing consulates.

agree that the United States should be devoting more resources to intelligence.

The technical explanation for putting the NFIP inside the defense budget is that, having decided to hide intelligence spending, the defense budget, being so large, is a good place in which to hide it. Also, probably four-fifths of NFIP programs are operated by military personnel, and hiding these programs among other defense programs simplifies the bookkeeping. For example, the National Security Agency is an NFIP program and its budget is ultimately overseen by the Director of Central Intelligence, but many of the people within NSA are uniformed military personnel; the same is true of the Defense Intelligence Agency. Apportioning funds to the NFIP from the defense budget is simply a matter of following an accounting procedure called a "crosswalk," in which the money in individual lines in the defense budget that actually belongs to the intelligence community is transferred to NFIP program managers.

Probably the main reason the NFIP is contained inside the defense budget, however, is historical. As we have seen, many national intelligence activities—SIGINT and aerial reconnaissance, for example—were originally carried out by the military services and were taken over by the Director of Central Intelligence only after the modern intelligence community was created. It was much simpler to leave intelligence activities in the defense budget and delegate authority over them to the DCI (whose authority over intelligence programs carried out by military personnel was ambiguous at the time in any case) rather than to remove these programs from the Department of Defense and then redistribute them throughout the federal budget for the sake of secrecy.

Whatever the reasons for keeping the intelligence budget inside the defense budget, one key result is that pressure on the defense spending almost always results in indirect pressure on the intelligence budget. When defense spending is cut, defense officials ask intelligence officials to take their "fair share" of the cut.

To understand why, suppose that the Secretary of Defense, in making his initial budget proposal to the administration, asks for $300 billion for the next fiscal year. This figure would include the secret NFIP budget that, purely for the sake of illustration, let us assume is $20 billion. Thus, in this case the Defense Department actually hopes to spend $280 billion on military programs. Now, suppose the Office of Management and Budget tells the Secretary of Defense that the defense budget cannot exceed $285 billion (including the secret NFIP budget), or 5 percent less than the secretary originally requested.

The Secretary of Defense would have an incentive to ask the Director of Central Intelligence to reduce his own budget request for intelligence by 5 percent. If the defense budget is cut 5 percent, and the defense budget is required to carry an unaltered NFIP, then, it can be argued, the Defense Department has been hit twice—once by the defense cut and once to make additional room for the constant-sized intelligence budget. In the illustration above, for example, the NFIP's "fair share" of the 5 percent cut in the original $300 billion defense budget request would have been $1 billion. If the NFIP were not reduced by this much, the Defense Department would have to absorb the loss. As a result, "true" defense spending—that is, the defense budget that is not really the NFIP—would be $260 billion rather than $261 billion. To appreciate the Defense Secretary's perspective, remember that this additional $1 billion would buy about one-third of an aircraft carrier, three strategic bombers, or about four hundred main battle tanks.

The same thing can occur on Capitol Hill. If the House Armed Services Committee authorizes less money for the defense budget than the President requests, its members are likely to ask the House Permanent Select Committee on Intelligence to make a proportionate reduction in its authorization for the NFIP, since the defense authorization must contain the intelligence authorization. If the House Intelligence Committee does not, then the impact of any reductions in authorized defense programs will be magnified.

SOME IMMEDIATE ISSUES

Trends in Intelligence Spending
and the Planning Problem

With these links between defense and intelligence spending, it should not be surprising that fluctuations in the intelligence community's budget have followed fluctuations in the defense budget. The historical relationship between the two are illustrated in the accompanying diagrams. Figure 6.1 depicts outlays for defense from 1950 to 1988 in inflation-adjusted dollars. As the chart indicates, the defense budget has reached three peaks during the postwar era: the buildup associated with the Korean War and the remobilization for the Cold War, the Vietnam War, and the buildup begun in the last year of the Carter administration and maintained until the mid-1980s under the Reagan administration. Most experts believe that defense spending will begin to decline as we enter the 1990s, reflecting the public's concern with the federal budget deficit and a general weakening of support for larger military budgets.

Now notice Figure 6.2, which depicts trends in U.S. intelligence spending and the distribution of the intelligence budget. (The precise amount of money the United States spends on intelligence activities is secret so dollar figures on the vertical axis have been omitted; this chart is, thus, an approximation that reflects what has been officially disclosed.) As can be seen, the intelligence budget has tended to shadow the defense budget: the intelligence budget grew in the early 1950s, mid-1960s, and early 1980s, and declined in the intervening years.

So long as defense spending is rising, as it was throughout the period from 1979 to 1985, the tie between intelligence and defense is not much of a constraint on intelligence planning. The problem occurs when defense spending falls, as seems likely to occur in the years immediately ahead.

One might argue that the United States needs to decide the total amount of money it can afford to spend on national security and then decide how much intelligence should be in the total mix of national security programs. Moreover, in an

143

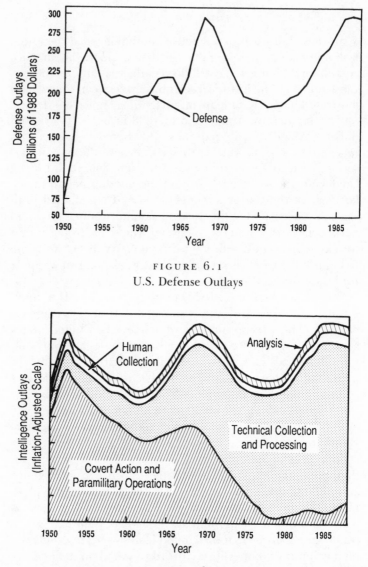

FIGURE 6.1
U.S. Defense Outlays

FIGURE 6.2
Distribution of Intelligence Outlays by Function

era of $200 billion government deficits, no part of the federal budget can be sacrosanct. But it does seem reasonable to make sure that funding decisions for intelligence are made in light of intelligence requirements rather than as some arbitrary proportion of the defense budget. Even though most intelligence spending is contained in the defense budget, intelligence is not just another defense program. The intelligence community has many other customers besides the armed services. This is especially true today, when intelligence support is required for such diverse tasks as carrying out foreign policy, monitoring arms control, developing effective trade and industrial development policies, and agricultural planning.

To be fair, all of the players who take part in the budget review for defense and intelligence—the Secretary of Defense, the DCI, OMB, and the members of the congressional committees—are aware of the situation, and, in the end, the "fair share" problem is resolved by political bargaining in which everyone generally gives a little ground. The real problem is that, when the intelligence budget is linked to defense spending levels, intelligence policy decisions are being made without referring to real intelligence requirements. The $1 billion intelligence cut portrayed in the previous illustration, for example, was simply an arbitrary byproduct of a decision to reduce defense spending. Indeed, the people cutting defense may not have intended to cut intelligence at all but inadvertantly did so by pressuring the defense budget.*

---

* Certainly the connection between the defense budget and the intelligence budget is not unique to the United States. In Great Britain, for instance, scientific and technical intelligence has often been financed through transfers from the armed services, and as the British Army and Navy faced tighter budgets, they were less willing to "subsidize" the intelligence services, and this constrained British scientific and technical intelligence. Peter Wright, former Assistant Director of MI-5 (British Counterintelligence), for example, has described the bargaining between MI-5 officials and the Admiralty to finance the development of electronic surveillance devices and countermeasures in the early 1950s. According to Wright, the MI-5 officials wanted to argue their own case in Cabinet and Parliamentary proceedings, but the need for secrecy made this impossible and they were compelled to

This problem is already beginning to appear. In the FY1986 budget, for example, defense spending (adjusted for inflation) experienced its first decline in seven years. That same year, intelligence also incurred what is euphemistically called in government circles "negative growth."[1]

There is no obvious reason why changes in intelligence spending should vary in step with the defense budget. Indeed, logically the opposite would seem true, since when we reduce defense spending, we probably need more intelligence in order to make the most of the military forces we have left. And, as we have already seen, the nondefense requirements for intelligence have been rising steadily, and meeting these requirements requires additional resources.

This potential budget squeeze is especially threatening because reducing the intelligence budget today would have an even greater impact on the actual intelligence product than in previous years. This is because the mix of programs within the intelligence budget has changed greatly in the past four decades.

Notice the historical distribution of intelligence outlays depicted in Figure 6.2. Two trends are immediately apparent: first, funds spent on programs for analysis and HUMINT have remained more or less constant and have always accounted for a rather small portion of the intelligence budget; second, the distribution of the rest of the budget has shifted significantly during the past forty years. Spending on covert action and paramilitary operations has fallen, while spending on technical collection and processing has climbed dramatically. This trend partly reflects a political decision—a decision to rely less on covert action in U.S. national security policy—and partly reflects the changing nature of how intelligence is produced.

During the 1950s and early 1960s, the United States car-

---

bargain or beg from the armed services. Wright claims that it was this "more than any other factor which contributed to the amateurism of British Intelligence in the immediate postwar era." See Peter Wright (with Paul Greengrass), *Spycatcher: The Candid Autobiography of a Senior Intelligence Officer* (New York: Viking Penguin, 1987), pp. 21–22.

ried out a wide range of large-scale covert actions programs. These operations included, for example, proprietary companies such as Civil Air Transport and Air America; full-scale guerrilla wars, such as that carried out by U.S.-backed Hmong fighters in Laos; a vigorous political action program of supporting parties and political movements abroad amenable to U.S. interests; and broadcasting companies, such as Radio Free Europe and Radio Liberty. Most of these programs were wound down by the mid-1970s, and covert action as a whole has been carried out on a smaller scale and has become more narrowly focused. As a result, covert action currently accounts for a much smaller part of the total intelligence budget.[2]

Meanwhile, the intelligence community has come to rely more and more on technical systems for collecting and processing data. The growth in spending for technical collection began in the 1950s (coinciding with the u-2 and sr-71 programs) and continued throughout the following decades. By the mid-1970s, programs for SIGINT collection and processing, cryptography, satellite reconnaissance, and other complex, expensive technical activities accounted for the bulk of the intelligence budget. The net result is that today almost any significant reduction in the intelligence budget will inevitably result in a significant reduction in the quantity and quality of the information that the community is able to provide its clientele. Unlike the 1970s, when some of these cuts could be taken out of covert action programs, today there is little slack.

The reliance on technology also creates other problems. One is that the high-tech systems on which the intelligence communities rely so heavily these days are notoriously sensitive to stops and starts in funding. As most defense analysts know, the prices of fighter aircraft and missiles escalate sharply when their programs are modified in midstream or stretched out to accommodate smaller budgets. The same is true of high-tech intelligence systems.

Another problem is that as the intelligence community has turned to more complex (and more expensive) systems, it has also tended to operate fewer systems. So, where fifteen or twenty years ago a reconnaissance mission might have been carried out by ten satellites orbited over a period of four years, today the same mission might be carried out by a single satellite operated over a period of four years. This has lost the community considerable flexibility in coping with fluctuating budgets. It is more difficult to adjust to budget cuts when one is operating a few high-capability systems, as decisions have to be made in bigger units. For example, postponing an upgrade to a satellite system means doing without the additional capability for the entire four years the satellite is in operation. Eliminating a program often means eliminating an entire category of data that can be collected.

Reconciling the Problems of Secrecy and Planning

One way to break the arbitrary link between defense and intelligence would be to separate the NFIP budget from the defense budget and allow intelligence to be judged on its own merit. However, doing so would reveal the total amount of money being spent by the United States on intelligence, and this is a controversial issue.

Opponents make two main arguments against any measure that would reveal total U.S. intelligence spending. One—"the bulge in the python argument"—maintains that such disclosure would compromise security because foreign countries would be alerted to the start of any major new U.S. intelligence program by looking for growth in the budget. Looking at the intelligence budget plotted over five or ten years, one could, it is said, detect a new program by the bulge in the budget that would appear as the program is developed, built, and then deployed. Former DCI William Colby, for example, claims that revealing the total amount of money in the intelligence budget would have compromised the development and deployment of the U-2 aircraft in the 1950s.[3] Other individuals, though, counter by arguing that the U.S. intelligence program is sufficiently diversified today that such a "bulge" could not be identified with any particular program. Indeed, a number of approximations of total U.S. intelligence spending have already been leaked to the media, and the impact on the intelligence community appears to have been negligible. The second argument against separating intelligence funding into its own account is the "camel's nose under the tent" thesis: any disclosure of an aggregate figure for intelligence would inevitably lead to demands for additional information, which would eventually be granted and would thus compromise specific intelligence programs. Individuals who have taken this position point to the experience of the Atomic Energy Commission. In 1947, the AEC disclosed a single line item for U.S. spending on nuclear weapons programs; by 1974, this entry had been expanded to fifteen pages of funding information.[4]

Yet there are ways to insulate intelligence from fluctuations in defense spending without disclosing the amount of money the United States spends on intelligence. One way would be to retain *most* of the intelligence budget within defense, allow this part of the budget to continue to fluctuate with defense spending, and create a separate, unclassified line in the federal budget that could be used as a "surge tank" to compensate intelligence when defense budgets declined. The NFIP funds contained in the defense budget could fluctuate with other defense spending, and as long as the specific size of these programs remained secret, the unclassified account (one could label it "Supplementary National Intelligence") would offer no clue to the actual level of total intelligence spending.

To work, the unclassified account could be fairly small— under $1 billion—so as to be relatively noncontroversial in budget debates. Assume, for the sake of illustration, that intelligence spending equals 5 percent of the defense budget, or about $15 billion in the mid-1980s. If defense—about $300 billion in the 1980s—is cut 5 percent, then $750 million would have to be added to the "surge tank" account in order to hold intelligence spending constant. This account could also be managed in ways that would further obscure actual intelligence spending. For example, one could vary the rate at which funds authorized and appropriated in this budget line were paid out, so that the amount appearing in, say, the 1990 fiscal year budget might actually include funds that would be spent the following year.

This approach, interestingly enough, would resemble the method used by the Soviet Union to obscure how much it spends on defense. The Soviet national budget contains a line for "defense," but almost no one in the West believes that the paltry, relatively unchanging amount of rubles that appears in this line really represents what the Soviets spend on defense. Much of the Soviet defense budget is hidden in the accounts of various other ministries and in the Soviet space program. This ploy has been extremely effective: even though U.S. analysts have ample data on nondefense Soviet programs, the true level of Soviet defense spending remains one of the great intelligence controversies of our time.[5]

Matching Intelligence Demands and Funding

Oddly enough, the second step necessary for ensuring that intelligence funding matches our expectations for intelligence support would seem to be exactly the opposite of the first. Decoupling the intelligence budget from the defense budget is necessary in order to avoid imposing an arbitrary cap on intelligence spending. However, it is also necessary to ensure that when a new defense program or foreign policy is adopted and creates new requirements for intelligence, the intelligence community will have the resources needed to respond to these requirements. Or to put it another way, when the feasibility of Defense Program X or Foreign Policy Y depends on our having certain intelligence, we need to make sure that this intelligence either already exists or that new resources have been planned to provide it.

Few such linkages exist today, and so intelligence is often considered a "free good" (at least implicitly) by intelligence consumers. This creates two problems. First, consumers develop programs without investigating whether the intelligence necessary to make these systems work is actually available or, if it is not, whether it is even feasible. Second, as with most free goods, consumers often act as though there is no limit to the intelligence they can have.

For an example of how defense systems produce implicit requirements for intelligence, consider electronic countermeasure (ECM) systems. Most U.S. combat aircraft carry equipment that alerts the pilot when the aircraft is being scanned ("illuminated," to use the technical jargon) by enemy radar. These devices, which are sophisticated versions of the "fuzzbusters" many of us use in our cars to warn us of police radar on the highway, calculate the frequency and phase of the radar and, in the more advanced models, transmit signals that either jam or distort the enemy's radar receiver. The devices are often designed as pods to be mounted on the wing of an aircraft.

To build and operate an ECM system, one needs to know the characteristics of the opponent's radar. Otherwise, the designer of the system does not know what frequencies it should receive. It also helps to know the location of these radar systems and the usual pattern in which they are operated. And, since the Soviets can readjust their radars or deploy new models, this "electronic order of battle" must be updated periodically. All of this information must be provided by the intelligence community; otherwise, it is simply impossible to build or operate an ECM system.

So, whenever the Air Force or Navy decides to deploy a new ECM system, they are implicitly creating a new requirement for the U.S. intelligence community. In this case, the new requirement is having to supply the data on Soviet defense systems necessary to design the ECM system and update it periodically during its operational lifetime. Officials should know this additional long-term cost when deciding whether to build the ECM system, just as when deciding whether to buy a new bomber or destroyer, they consider associated lifetime expenses such as fuel and crew costs. Unfortunately, under current procedures, intelligence requirements usually are not provided for or even identified when the total cost of a new weapon system is being estimated.* Since the data for programming an ECM system is absolutely necessary for its operation, the best way to ensure that the costs for this intelligence are considered in the decision to buy an ECM system—and ensure that the necessary funds are set aside for the intelligence community—is to include them in the total authorization for the weapon. This way the money necessary for intelligence support could simply be transferred to the appropriate intelligence agency account when the necessary intelligence is prepared. This is virtually the same procedure used to pay other overhead costs today.

Electronic countermeasure systems are just one example of how intelligence costs can be overlooked. To appreciate how widespread this problem is, consider how many different weapons require regularly provided intelligence support. Cruise missiles require terrain contour or ground feature maps for their guidance systems; inertial guidance systems used in bombers, missiles, and submarines require data on regional variations in gravity; "smart" munitions require data on the signatures of their intended targets; and so on.

Foreign policy initiatives and other nonmilitary programs also impose intelligence costs. An arms control ceiling on ICBMs, for example, would require that the U.S. develop the intelligence systems necessary to count Soviet mobile missiles, such as the SS-24 and SS-25. A limit on missile throw-weight requires intelligence on the capabilities of Soviet missiles. An antidrug policy requires intelligence on the sources of nar-

* The one exception to this rule is mapping, charting, and geodesy ("MC&G"), which are prepared by the Defense Mapping Agency, an intelligence unit funded as a TIARA program within the Defense Department. Under rules adopted in the second term of the Reagan administration, the costs for maps required by a specific weapon must be written into the cost of the weapon system itself. For example, cruise missiles use a form of terrain-following radar to guide them to their targets; they therefore require a new ground contour map to be programmed into their guidance system computer whenever they are assigned a new target. These maps can be quite expensive, and the costs for this MC&G would, at least in future systems, be considered part of the total weapon system.

cotics and tactical intelligence on their shipment. In all of these cases, the policy fails or is rendered ineffective if the necessary intelligence has not been planned and/or cannot be funded.

Another way to link intelligence funding to intelligence demands is through the intelligence planning process. Intelligence decisions, like those of other government activities, are usually made in reference to *programs*—that is, just as the government decides whether to fund Health Care Program A or Weapon System B, it also decides whether to fund Intelligence Satellite C or Intelligence Computer D. Since the intelligence community itself is organized in terms of programs, this orientation is probably inescapable. The problem in reviewing the budget this way is that it does not tell the users of intelligence which intelligence systems they need. As a result, the intelligence consumers are unable to tell administration officials and legislators which systems they should support when priorities have to be set. For example, officials at the Arms Control and Disarmament Agency might not know that a certain computer NSA wants approved is essential to estimating Soviet ICBM throw-weight, and so they might not seek the opportunity to express their priority for the product. Certainly intelligence users are not required to indicate what they would be willing to forgo in order to retain that computer.

One solution for this problem is to prepare a set of documents parallel to the DCI's programmatic budget. These documents would break down the intelligence program into missions: verifying arms control agreements, providing data on Soviet weapons design, supplying intelligence to combat the international drug trade, etc. The analysis in the document would then describe how each mission was to be carried out under the DCI's plan and which programs were essential to the mission. Such an analysis would not guarantee a better allocation of intelligence funds, but if it were circulated through the government, intelligence users would be able to see which of their requirements were being met, and how, and indicate their intelligence priorities accordingly.

Top intelligence officials spend much, if not most, of their time worrying about and coping with such budget constraints. While the arcane procedures of government accounting may seem far removed from "real" intelligence problems, the fact remains that unfunded intelligence programs produce no intelligence.

PERSONNEL

A second major problem that will face the intelligence community in the coming years is the recruitment, training, retention, and retirement of intelligence personnel. Personnel policy is critical because so many aspects of intelligence performance translate into personnel issues. The quality of intelligence analysis, for instance, depends on whether the community can attract talented analysts. Crisis management depends on the ability of collection managers to deal with a wide range of rapidly changing problems. Surge capacity depends on the ability of case officers to move from one country or subject of current interest to another. Maintaining security and protecting secrets is in large part a matter of screening out would-be penetrators during the recruitment process and ensuring that those accepted for employment are protected from terrorist threats or blackmail and recruitment attempts by foreign intelligence services.

Some of our major personnel concerns are detailed in the following pages:

Personal Security

An unfortunate fact today is the growing exposure of intelligence officers to all kinds of dangers. A career in intelligence has usually been assumed to carry some amount of risk—U.S. intelligence personnel have always been warned of the dangers of provocation while traveling in the Soviet bloc—but today these risks have grown. Also, they are being encountered in places where they were absent before. For example, previously it was assumed that only intelligence officers abroad would be faced with physical danger. Today even office buildings used by the intelligence community in Washington, D.C., are protected against the terrorist threat, and even analysts on vacation abroad now need to take at least a few preventive measures to protect themselves and their families.

Similarly, the threat of recruitment by foreign intelligence services was previously perceived largely as a Soviet threat. Recent espionage cases suggest, though, that the Soviets are making greater use of the Polish, Czech, and East German intelligence services, and this multiplies the number and variety of threats intelligence officers must recognize. Indeed, as the Jonathan Jay Pollard case illustrated, the new threat can come from directions totally unsuspected up to now; Pollard, a naval intelligence analyst convicted of passing classified U.S. intelligence to a foreign intelligence service, was recruited by Israel.

The Talent Pool in the United States

Of all of the personnel problems the intelligence community will face in the coming years, the most difficult to solve is likely to be maintaining the base of talent the community requires to carry out its mission. As we have already observed, much of the work of the intelligence community is highly specialized and requires exceptional creativity. In addition to specialists in Soviet missile design, the community will probably also require analysts familiar with the language, religion, and culture of Southwest Asia, analysts who understand both basics of the microelectronics and metallurgy industry and the economic constraints that will shape the spread of this industry in the Third World, analysts expert in the European, Japanese, and Chinese programs for space exploration and exploitation, and analysts who understand the party politics and new social movements that might fragment the Western Alliance. It is also safe to say that some of the most pressing analytic skills the community will require are precisely those we cannot even foresee at this time.

The difficulty in developing these skills is more subtle than one might think—and harder to solve. The intelligence community is limited by the pool of talent available in the United States as a whole. Obviously maintaining the national talent pool is beyond the capabilities of the intelligence community. This is the job of the nation's educational system. Unfortunately, the relationship between the intelligence community and academia has become strained during the past two decades, beginning in 1967 with the disclosure in *Ramparts* magazine that the CIA had been subsidizing the foreign activities of the National Student Association. Relations soured further with the disclosure of illegal intelligence activities during the 1970s, so that by the end of the decade intelligence agencies often were unable even to have recruitment representatives on campus, a prerogative allowed almost any other major private and public employer.[6]

The tension between the intelligence and the academic communities is ironic, considering that the modern intelligence community traces its origins to academia. As noted earlier, William Donovan, father of the OSS, established what became the predecessor of the Directorate of Intelligence and the National Intelligence Council as a special office in the Library of Congress. The discipline of comparative political studies in the United States is based in large part on the area analyses carried out by the Office of Strategic Services in World War II, and the OSS analysts who returned to academia after the war helped form the basis of the higher education system that trained the flood of students resulting from the postwar education boom.[7]

Of course, some academics attack the basic legitimacy of intelligence activities, and these individuals will probably always object to any relationship between the intelligence community and academia. Yet even some academics who have no philosophical objections to the activities of the intelligence community have raised legitimate questions concerning the relationship between intelligence and academia that must be answered in the period ahead.

For instance, one of these questions concerns whether academics serving as part-time consultants to the intelligence community should be permitted to keep these relationships secret. If they do, and these relationships are later disclosed, then even the nongovernment research the academician carried out while the relationship existed might be considered suspect. Also, the academician's colleagues or students might also be suspected of having ties to the intelligence community or of being used unwittingly by U.S. intelligence agencies. In addition to antagonizing professors who prefer not to be linked to intelligence, this suspicion can cause real problems for other academicians who might want to carry out research in the Soviet Union or many countries in the Third World, and especially for those academicians who happen to be colleagues of the professor with the consulting relationship.

It is difficult to resolve this question on a purely philosophical basis and decide whether an invasion of privacy is justified in this case, but the problem can be addressed in more practical terms. Since U.S. intelligence depends on the viability of the educational system for its pool of talent, it seems that it would be in the long-term interest of the intelligence community to respect the norms that academe has found essential to its existence. In general, this means any research grants or student financial assistance stemming from intelligence agencies must be provided openly, and the results of such research conducted at colleges and universities must be disclosed as freely as other research.

Recruitment

In the mid-1970s, many people were surprised to find large display advertisements by the CIA and NSA in the classified section (an unintended irony) of leading newspapers. These advertisements sought recruits for the intelligence services and reflected both the difficulties the intelligence community faced at the time in finding adequate numbers of applicants and the desire of intelligence officials to reach out to draw new blood from a wider cross-section of society. The community has much less difficulty recruiting today, though the advertisements have continued to appear.

Such advertisements are perhaps the most visible signs of the efforts that the intelligence community is now making to recruit new talent, even though, according to almost all accounts, such wide-net approaches are not very productive when one considers the effort required to sort through the flood of applications that such advertisements produce—according to public reports, some eighteen to twenty thousand in recent years. But they do reflect the general approach that the intelligence community has begun to take in recruiting personnel.

Recruitment in almost every intelligence agency is currently highly centralized in a department or an office of personnel. Staff members from line offices may be assigned to the personnel division on rotation, but the offices and recruitment programs are still under the supervision of support personnel, rather than line officers. Thus, intelligence recruitment, like the planning of analysis, is carried out "Soviet style" and suffers many of the disadvantages of a centralized economy.

A conversation with almost anyone who has applied for a job in the intelligence community will reveal that at least a year, and often more, can pass between the time a recruit applies for a position and when he or she finally is either brought on board or turned down for employment. The primary reasons for the lengthy processing time are bottlenecks at key stages of the recruitment process. Most of these bottlenecks have to do with security—in particular, conducting background investigations and polygraph exams.

This imposes a disadvantage on the community, which must compete with private industry and other government departments for the same talent pool. Many recruits have been reluctant to wait a year or more for a new job that often cannot be described in detail. Such delays can be an effective deterrent to even the most highly motivated candidate. Unfortunately, the resources necessary to improve security screening have traditionally had a low priority. In critical situations, such as in the late 1970s, when additional Farsi linguists were needed, the process is usually accelerated when it is brought to the attention of a higher official. But the routine procedure, with its delays summed over the entire community, clearly acts as a major drag in recruiting top-flight analysts and case officers.

One solution that has been tried by some agencies is to put more of the burden of recruitment on the line offices rather than a central personnel department, letting missile engineers use their expertise and contacts to find new missile engineers, economists to find economists. The CIA already has taken some steps in this direction, for example, by allowing line analysts to take rotating tours of duty as recruiters. This, however, still has the effect of detaching the recruitment process from the offices that have the immediate need for the personnel.

Rather than rotating analysts through personnel, it may be more effective simply to make recruitment one of the duties of being a manager in an analysis division, encouraging these managers to maintain their ties to professional organizations and academia in order to spot new talent. One might re-create a modern version of the "old school network" used by the CIA in the 1950s and 1960s. This network had the reputation of being biased in favor of white males (possibly deserved, but probably no more than similar networks in business or even academia at the time), but there is no reason why such a bias must exist, and informal networks could even reinforce affirmative action measures if used effectively. So, instead of soliciting 150 applications from a mass audience, accepting 10 recruits, and finding only 2 on the job three years later, one would solicit 15 applications, accept 10, and find 7 on the job within two years.

Another problem of personnel policy lies in the specialization required of many intelligence positions. Not only does this make filling these positions difficult; it also creates major headaches for managing personnel and retaining them once they have been recruited.

A classic illustration of this problem occurred during and after the Vietnam War. During the war, the intelligence community had problems finding experts in Indochina quickly enough to meet its rapidly growing requirements. After the United States withdrew from the war, the community was saddled with more Indochina experts than it needed.[8] This is one more example of the "surge capacity" problem in intelligence. Just as technical assets have to be sufficiently flexible to be shifted from one target to another, so do intelligence personnel. And just as the specialization required of technical intelligence systems complicates the planning of surge capacity, the specialization required of intelligence personnel produces similar complications.

But in the case of personnel, specialization leads to problems other than just that of flexibility. Specialization can also lead to problems in retention. Because intelligence personnel often have esoteric skills and a high level of training, they often have a considerable number of employment opportunities outside the intelligence community. The background and skills intelligence personnel acquire while working in the community can also make them a highly sought-after commodity by private industry or government agencies with faster promotion rates.

For example, the most common "skill" a person acquires by working in intelligence is a security clearance. Cleared personnel are in great demand among government contractors. In part this is because initial background investigations can be costly—usually about $1,800 per case. Obviously, contractors prefer that someone else assume this cost, if possible. Even more important, the time required to clear a new employee can result in costly delays for a project. The typical investigation for a new employee can require nine months to a year, while individuals leaving the intelligence community for the private sector can usually have their clearances transferred within a week or two.[9]

Because its people do have such marketable skills, the intelligence community sometimes has difficulty in retaining some of its most valuable people. Keeping cleared clerical staff is a frequent problem, for example, as private corporations are almost always able to outbid the community in the salaries they offer. The problem is even more apparent, however, for intelligence officers in their late thirties or early forties and having ten to fifteen years of experience—often the most productive individuals in an organization. The best of these intelligence officers will have peaked out at the top levels of the government pay scales. In other cases, they may find that the only way they can continue to earn higher salaries is to leave their job as a working analyst, engineer, or case officer and assume a position in management. The CIA has tried to address this problem by creating more "supergrade" positions for senior analysts and case officers, but these positions are still quite limited, and DIA, INR, and most other agencies lag behind in any case.

MAKING THE BUREAUCRACY WORK

Many of the problems of the intelligence community are a direct result of its being a bureaucracy. Max Weber defined a bureaucracy as an organization with these three characteristics:

— An orientation toward carrying out a particular mission. Few bureaucracies are "all-purpose"; the CIA produces intelligence, the Army fights battles on land, and the EPA regulates producers of polluting substances.

— A hierarchical structure, with specific responsibilities assigned to subunits within the organization. In the CIA, branch chiefs report to division chiefs, division chiefs report to office chiefs, office chiefs report to the Deputy Director for Intelligence, and the DDI reports to the Director of Central Intelligence.

— A membership that is evaluated on the basis of "objective" measures rather than "market" measures. Intelligence analysts are not penalized if policymakers fail to read the latest NIE; instead, analysts are promoted on the basis of fitness report results and seniority.[10]

The term "bureaucratic" has assumed an especially unfavorable connotation in recent years. It is often taken to be synonymous with "stultified." But bureaucratic organizations meet a vital need. Bureaucracies are usually more stable than private firms, if only because they do not have to worry about market competition. This may leave them poorly equipped to innovate and respond to new demands, but it also makes them well-suited for routine operations that one would not want to leave at risk in the open market.

Many intelligence functions fit this description. Indeed, the intelligence community carries out "routine" operations remarkably well—producing overhead photographs on a regular basis, turning out a daily summary of signals intelligence, and maintaining data bases, for example. The intelligence "utility companies" that produce these mass-market products, however, are often not as good at responding to new requirements, unusual situations, or special requests.

Stansfield Turner, for example, tells a humorous anecdote of how, when he first arrived at the CIA, President Carter, apparently trying to see how quickly the intelligence community could perform, asked for a satellite photograph of a battlefield in a war that was taking place between two Third World countries. Turner said he would get the photograph immediately and passed the order on to his assistants. The first response was simply to let the request slide; Turner repeated the order. But weeks went by, and the representatives from the satellite imagery agency kept telling Turner that they were having problems. Meanwhile, the President was beginning to chide Turner at their twice-weekly meetings. Eventually Turner was able to find some photographs taken by a military attaché that met the requirement.[11]

Later, Turner found out that the satellites had not even been targeting the battlefield. Early in the war, analysts had found that they could monitor the progress of the war better by targeting the approaches through which the armies were transporting their equipment rather than the battlefield itself. The equipment was concentrated in convoys when it was being transported and was dispersed and hidden once it was in the battle area. The satellite had thus been programmed to photograph the approaches. So, when the inquiry from Turner arrived, asking whether anything had been spotted on the battlefield, the answer was, naturally, "not at this time."

Critics of bureaucracy would cite this as a typical case of recalcitrant, unresponsive behavior. Yet, in reality, the agencies responsible for satellite imagery regularly provide thousands of images that meet the requirements of consumers across the national security community—a remarkable feat. In other words, they are meeting the demands of the mass market; their problem is just that they are poorly suited to responding to tailored, specific requests. Yet consider the consequences if the agency responsible for satellite imagery had to respond regularly to the off-the-cuff requests of high-level customers such as the President. There is little doubt that they could, but they would probably have to compromise the large, efficient organization and operating rules that make it possible today for them to meet the bulk of the demands from their wider clientele.

Thus, the problem: how do we maintain the stability and efficiency of a bureaucracy for routine intelligence operations, while still providing a means for the innovation and flexibility that intelligence requires? Several approaches have been attempted. The main problems lie in determining when a particular approach should be tried and how to implement it.

For example, one technique is to create small, independent organizations within the larger intelligence bureaucracy and assign them specific missions to carry out and then leave the actual planning of the operation to the organizations themselves. Small bureaucracies are usually more flexible and innovative, especially when they are young. Their risk is that they have a higher probability of failing completely when their flexible, innovative approaches do not work as planned. Since the responsibilities of these organizations can be limited, though, so can the costs.

This was the approach used, for example, by IBM to develop its new personal computers. Though a firm, IBM resembles a government bureaucracy in many respects. It is known for its dependability but also its internal regimentation. Some IBM managers feared that this would prevent it from competing effectively in the rough-and-tumble market that was opening up for the personal computer, and so it created a separate organization for this mission. While IBM would not reform its main corporate structure along these guidelines, the strategy was successful in getting the company into the personal computer market.

The intelligence community has used similar methods on occasion. The best example is probably the Lockheed Skunk Works, which has become virtually synonymous with the small-group approach in business and was responsible for developing intelligence aircraft such as the U-2 and SR-71. In the analytic community, the Office of National Estimates, when it was first created, could also be cited as an example of this strategy, as could the special task forces the community has on occasion created to analyze specific issues.

Another approach to dealing with the challenges of bureaucracy is through the use of outside contractors for some analytic tasks. Private consultants and contractors have received much publicity in recent years (usually bad), but a brief review of the economic factors that lead to the existence and the use of consultants will show why they are necessary to an organization that faces the kind of changing demands that the intelligence community must address.

Caps on federal salaries limit what an intelligence analyst or manager can earn to about $71,000. A new analyst with a Ph.D. will typically be a GS-9 and will earn about $23,000 per year, and in ten to fifteen years, he or she could become a senior analyst, usually a GS-15, who today earns about $54,000 per year. These salaries are below what top-level managers and specialists with valuable engineering, technical, or analytic skill can earn in the private sector, but, in return, the federal employee receives job security and considerable nonsalary benefits.

Simply looking at the pay structure, it seems as though the intelligence community, like other bureaucracies, aims at attracting people who are willing to forgo salary for security. The community seems to be shying away from risk-takers, or those willing to take a chance for a big potential payoff, as well as the highly skilled, expensive specialist. Those who want to earn more, albeit with less security, or those willing to take chances on new ideas have considerable incentives to leave the community for the private sector. (The fact that the intelligence community is, in fact, *not* filled with mediocre personnel says much about the intrinsic reward intelligence personnel apparently find in their work.)

Fortunately, intelligence officers who leave the community for better opportunities do not just disappear. They often either become independent consultants or join corporate contractors. Either way, their talent remains on the market, if the government is willing to pay for it.

This may seem cynical, but actually it provides the intelligence community the ability to limit risks, carry out its day-to-day tasks, and still obtain the skilled, high-priced talent it requires for certain operations. Private contractors have always been used by the intelligence community. Scouts hired by the cavalry in the American West during the 1800s were intelligence consultants of a sort, as was the "dollar-a-year man" who donated his expertise to an intelligence agency in the 1940s and 1950s. (Possibly the most notable of these was Edwin Land of Polaroid fame, who, it has been said, often refused compensation even for his personal expenses during the two decades he assisted the intelligence community in developing overhead imagery systems.) By contracting out certain assignments, the intelligence community is able to acquire the skills it needs but cannot or should not afford to retain permanently.

Many government agencies are increasingly using their own staffs primarily for management and contracting out the technical tasks for which they are responsible. For example, the Environmental Protection Agency contracts firms to monitor compliance with pollution standards, and the Department of Transportation contracts out most of the research it uses to develop safety standards. The intelligence community has been doing this, too, though not so extensively as agencies such as EPA or DOT. Again, the question is one of how this management tool is used and whether it is used effectively.

If policies governing consulting in the intelligence community can be faulted for anything, it is only that the true rationale for hiring outside help is often not considered when making policy. It is impossible to determine with publicly available data how efficiently consultants are used, but it is likely that the use of consultants usually is not considered in the overall planning of U.S. intelligence. One reason for believing this is that funds for consultants are usually among the first items cut when agency budgets are squeezed. In effect, one might be sacrificing the most specialized (and, thus, many of the most critical) activities of an agency. Or, the reverse may true: consultants are often considered a "bonus" or a "luxury" that an agency hires when it is flush with money, regardless of whether their activities are essential to the agency's mission.

Ideally, one would want to identify core missions that must be supported by full-time, permanent employees and supplement these personnel with a more flexible workforce. A former DCI gave an example of how this might be done when interviewed by the authors: the CIA, obviously, needs a full-time analyst to monitor countries such as Egypt or South Africa; but what about Ghana, or Senegal, or Burundi? When an official wants an assessment of Senegal, he or she does not want a dilettante doing the assessment, but it would be inefficient to hire an analyst who specialized in Senegalese affairs, and especially a subspecialization such as western Senegalese agricultural affairs. However, the CIA could pay a consultant a retainer to stay current on Senegal affairs at a high level of detail, reading the native Senegalese newspapers every day and perhaps visiting the country once a year. Then, when information on Senegal is required, the CIA would be prepared.

Budgets, personnel, and organizational matters will probably never be as interesting to the outsider as moles and covert action. Certainly they will never attract as much attention in the media. Yet these issues are the ones that will determine whether the intelligence community is effective in the years ahead, and if U.S. leaders are to have the intelligence they need, then these are the topics that they will need to address.

SEVEN

The Challenge Ahead and Lessons from Experience

In the decades since Sherman Kent published *Strategic Intelligence*, the U.S. intelligence community has succeeded in thoroughly transforming the craft of intelligence. It has developed and routinized the process of producing sophisticated, comphrehensive estimates. It has developed remarkable technical collection systems such as the U-2 and reconnaissance satellites. And it has assembled a body of human talent that can only be described as unique. On the other hand, as we have seen, the intelligence community has also experienced some major failures during this time: the inability to predict the deployment of missiles to Cuba, the escalation of foreign oil prices, the Yom Kippur War, and the fall of the Shah; overestimates of the Soviet military buildup in the 1950s and underestimates in the 1960s; and a lack of access to the inner political circles of totalitarian states all come readily to mind. The remainder of the twentieth century promises, if anything, to be even more challenging.

One measure of the increasing difficulty of the intelligence mission is reflected in the tenure of the Director of Central Intelligence. Since 1948, when Kent wrote *Strategic Intelligence*, twelve different individuals have held the post of Director of Central Intelligence—an average tenure of just three and a half years, and this would be shorter still were it not for the relatively long terms of Allen Dulles and William Casey. Moreover, the DCI has more often than not left office with at least some controversy following him, whether in the form of an intelligence failure (Dulles), misbehavior or alleged misbehavior on the part of the intelligence community (Helms, Colby, Casey), or disagreement among senior administration officials over the DCI's role in national security decision making and control of the intelligence budget (Schlesinger, Turner).

Another indication of the difficulty of the intelligence mission emerges from the memoirs of retired presidents and leading foreign policy officials. Despite the many documented successes of the intelligence community, there is, with just a few exceptions, scarcely a positive mention of a Director of Central Intelligence in such books. Usually the DCI or CIA is mentioned in the context of an unsuccessful intelligence operation or the failure of the intelligence community to anticipate events.*

Some of the difficulties that lie ahead will be a result of intelligence requirements that will continue to expand at an accelerating pace—usually faster than the resources allotted to meet them. Some difficulties will be traceable to traditional problems inherent to the "craft of intelligence": leadership, planning, organization, clandestine collection, and analysis. Others will be the result of problems common to any bureaucratic institution and democratic political system and may be beyond the ability of even the best intelligence officials to master. And yet other challenges will be related to the organizational and budgetary problems of the government as a whole.

Can the U.S. intelligence community meet these challenges?

We think that it can. Despite the difficulty of the challenge, the intelligence community has at least three important strengths on which to draw in the years ahead.

The first strength is the acceptance today by U.S. officials and the American public of intelligence as an essential part

---

* For example, consider Richard Nixon's account of his reaction to the overthrow of Prince Sihanouk of Cambodia by Lon Nol in 1970: "Lon Nol's coup came as a complete surprise. The CIA had received no indication that the opposition to Sihanouk had gone so far. 'What the hell do those clowns do out there in Langley?' I asked Bill Rogers impatiently." See Richard Nixon, *RN: The Memoirs of Richard Nixon* (New York: Grosset & Dunlap, 1978).

of a national security policy. This fact may seem trivial at first, but remember that such was not always the case. Just fifty or sixty years ago, the Secretary of State could dismantle the Cipher Bureau on grounds that spying, even for the sake of national security, was wrong. Similarly, up until World War II, legislators were apt to cut funds earmarked for intelligence, claiming that intelligence programs were a superfluous luxury, and military and foreign policy officials would scarcely object. In this atmosphere, the intelligence community often was best off when it was simply ignored.

Today, in contrast, officials and legislators are in virtually unanimous agreement that intelligence is vital to American national security. Current debates focus not on whether we want intelligence but rather on how much we can afford and how the production of intelligence can best be carried out. With this legitimacy, intelligence is able today to compete with other interests for resources in debates over public policy. The task for intelligence officials is no longer to justify why the United States needs intelligence but rather to present a coherent plan for intelligence that is based on efficient management and clearly defined national priorities.

The second strength on which the intelligence community can draw is—odd as it may seem to some—oversight, and especially oversight by the legislative branch. Even though some debate still remains over how best to conduct congressional oversight of intelligence, oversight is accepted in principle by both the Congress and the intelligence community. As one leading official has observed, nearly two-thirds of those now working in the intelligence community began their careers after 1976, when the current oversight mechanisms were enacted, and know no other way of doing business.[1] Similarly, few legislators today would suggest that there are still matters dealing with intelligence that should be totally hidden from the legislative branch—as did some legislators as recently as fifteen years ago.[2]

Developing effective measures for oversight was a vital step because it was necessary in order to reconcile secret intelligence with democracy. If the oversight system had not been established, then the intelligence community would have remained an anomaly in the government. Critics could reasonably argue that a secret intelligence community had no place in American democracy, or that the community was out of control. Once acceptable oversight mechanisms existed, these arguments were for the most part deflated.

Institutionalizing oversight has also paid off by making congressional intervention into intelligence affairs constructive. It is inevitable that Congress will feel obliged to assert itself when an intelligence failure occurs; the constituents demand it. Unfortunately, as recently as the 1970s, Congress lacked both an outlet for its concerns about intelligence affairs and an effective lever for improving intelligence. As a result, oversight consisted of an ineffective process in which officials would neglect intelligence most of the time, be motivated into action only after something had gone awry, and then move in to "bayonet the wounded." Assuming the oversight process works as designed (and, admittedly, this has not always been the case), Congress today has the opportunity to educate itself about intelligence affairs, monitor the community as a routine practice, and take action to ensure better performance in the future when things go wrong.

Furthermore, oversight has provided the intelligence community "sponsors" in the legislative branch. As in the case of other agencies in government, oversight has enabled the intelligence community to develop advocates in Congress who understand intelligence requirements and who can articulate the case for intelligence activities. Of course, congressional oversight also carries the potential costs of inefficient pork barrel projects, logrolling, and "micromanagement." But these risks are inherent in any application of democratic rule, and they are easily outweighed by the costs the community has incurred when oversight has been lacking (or evaded).

The third asset the U.S. intelligence community enjoys is its ability to draw on the American private sector, especially through its special relationship with private industry and academia. This relationship ensures the community access to the top talent and the latest technology the United States has available. The potential costs of losing this connection were made abundantly clear in the 1970s, when the relationship between the community and academia was severely strained, and the community began to lose its access to the talent and support it requires to carry out its mission. The access of CIA recruiters to campuses is as vital as access to foreign sources of information, and the same degree of care needs to be taken to ensure that this access is not lost.

In addition to these three basic strengths, the intelligence community also has one additional tactical advantage that will enable it to deal with the challenges that are appearing on the horizon: predictability. The challenges the intelligence community will face in the years ahead may be difficult to solve, but, for the most part, they are at least foreseeable. Most of these challenges will be a continuation of trends we are witnessing today. In sum, they include:

— serving a growing number of consumers demanding intelligence and an increasing range of subjects they want analyzed within ever-shortening deadlines;

— coping with a tighter intelligence budget, where little real growth can be expected;

— planning and developing both technical and personnel requirements to address problems and subjects far into the future.

Sherman Kent concluded *Strategic Intelligence* with a section on "lessons from experience," in which he distilled what he had learned from his oss days in World War II about managing and providing intelligence to the national security community. Similarly, the record of intelligence operations during the past four decades suggest some general guidelines for ensuring effective intelligence to meet the challenges ahead.

1. Successful intelligence requires success at every step in the intelligence cycle. Possibly the single most important lesson is that the intelligence product depends on the intelligence process: one weak link can cause a total failure. Expert analysts are useless if they do not focus on the problems that concern intelligence consumers most and present their product in a form suited to the consumer's needs. Analysis is itself impossible if no data is available because collection efforts have failed. Modern collection systems, despite their remarkable abilities, cannot be designed appropriately if the planning process does not identify the most lucrative and highest-priority intelligence targets. Moreover, resources are always limited, so intelligence planners must choose whether to spend money on analysts, collection systems, processing, or some combination. It is impossible to determine the best mix without considering the intelligence cycle as a whole.

Even so, it is interesting that most analyses of intelligence failures seem to focus on isolated problems in just one part of the intelligence cycle. One study, for example, might demonstrate how an assessment erred because of faulty assumptions. Another study might examine the effects of disinformation or deception. Yet another might consider the effects of espionage and the compromise of sources and methods. And still another might blame the policymaker for ignoring warnings or refusing to bring intelligence into the policy process at the right point in time. Each of these studies (some of which the authors themselves have conducted) may be valuable, but they miss a key point: effective intelligence means effectiveness at each step of the intelligence cycle.*

2. Intelligence systems are most effective when they are planned and funded to respond to what intelligence consumers want to know.
This point may seem obvious, but intelligence planners sometimes lose sight of their primary mission: meeting the specific needs of the officials who use intelligence. This kind of disconnection can occur throughout the intelligence cycle, but it is most apparent in the case of collection systems, which ac-

---

* To show just how many different things can go wrong in intelligence and how difficult the process of producing intelligence can be, we have summarized in Appendix A the kinds of failures that are possible at each step in the intelligence cycle, citing examples discussed in this book that illustrate the problem.

count for most of the intelligence budget. For example, intelligence planners may develop a system to monitor Warsaw Pact forces without establishing just what types of information U.S. military commanders on the Central Front require. Or, to give another example, well-meaning intelligence officers may recruit an excellent human source on military planning in a foreign country when it is economic intelligence officials back home want most urgently.

These planning failures do not occur because intelligence officials simply do not care about the needs of their clientele. Almost without exception, they do. However, the national security community is so large that linkages between intelligence planners and intelligence consumers can easily break down. Moreover, intelligence technology has developed so quickly that there are always more options for collection systems than we can afford. This is why intelligence officials need better methods to make sure that they know what intelligence consumers really need, and—just as important—what these consumers would do without if forced to make a choice.

The intelligence community's current planning procedures—the "requirements process," with its KIQs, NITs, DCID 1/2, and so on—have not always been successful in linking planners and consumers. Generally, the requirements process works well for tasking collection systems once they are deployed but not as well in deciding which system should be acquired. One problem is simply that intelligence analysts and intelligence consumers are poorly represented in the meetings where these decisions are made. Decisions regarding future collection systems tend to be made by the operators of current systems. In effect, each existing collection system has a built-in corps of lobbyists ready to promote it (and its next-generation successor) as the answer to any and all requirements.

Another problem with the current planning system is that documents such as NITs and DCID 1/2 only identify intelligence targets or missions; they do not have to explain how these missions will be carried out. Also, intelligence planners do not have to say what missions they will *not* be able to carry out because other missions have been assigned higher priority. As a result, the difficult choices that limited resources force intelligence planners to make are not obvious, and thus they are not always exposed to serious criticism. The overall effect is that intelligence consumers have few opportunities to evaluate and comment on the plans and priorities of the intelligence community. The intelligence community has occasionally attempted to take a more "mission-oriented" approach, as in the case of the Intelligence Capabilities Plan and the National Intelligence Strategy, and these efforts do improve the opportunity that intelligence consumers have to make their priorities known. But these efforts have been sporadic.

Some steps that could improve this situation include:

— increasing the access of analysts and intelligence consumers to the collection planning process, providing clearances as necessary, and increasing the representation of analysts and consumers on collection-planning staffs;

— regularly surveying the missions that the intelligence community must carry out and establishing their priority in a plan to carry out these missions;

— submitting the resulting plan to intelligence consumers for comment and letting the consumers know which of their intelligence requirements will be met and which will not.

3. Intelligence analysis must respond to the specific requirements of specific consumers. There is no doubt that, when instructed, the intelligence community can provide analysis in precisely the form and exactly the level of detail that a specific consumer needs. For the most part, however, intelligence analysis is tied to formal production plans, and these do not always respond to the needs of intelligence consumers. It is revealing that when intelligence planners want to get a product for a high-priority consumer in a hurry, they usually make an end-run around the annual production plan and submit the request directly to a National Intelligence Officer or some other high-ranking analyst.

Improving the intelligence community's responsiveness to its consumers would require some significant changes in the planning procedures the DDI, INR, and other analytical components of the community currently follow. Some of these changes could include:

— using analysis production plans primarily to guide research rather than to schedule specific intelligence products;

— using specific requests for information from intelligence consumers to schedule products;

— developing polished, on-the-shelf studies only after several intelligence consumers make similar requests for a particular assessment, demonstrating that a demand for such a standardized product exists;

— making greater use of direct contacts between analysts and intelligence consumers for planning production.

The intelligence community already devotes considerable resources to short-notice products for specific consumers. However, it does not plan as effectively as it might to provide this form of support.

Analysts require an opportunity to carry out in-depth research projects in order to develop a complete understanding of the events they must cover. Much of the education of an analyst consists of what the analyst learns by carrying out research necessary for a detailed report. Short, pithy, intelligence briefs for specific consumers usually require an analyst to live off of his or her "intellectual capital," as there simply is no time for much research when writing such a piece.

The in-depth studies that the intelligence community produces on subjects such as the design philosophy of Soviet naval combatants or trends in the organization of Chinese weapons manufacturers are high-quality publications that often cannot be found anywhere else. Unfortunately, the demand for such detailed studies by intelligence consumers is

relatively small, since few officials have the time to read trea-
tises. As a result, these publications often go unread and, indeed, it often seems that there are two main beneficiaries of
such studies: the analyst who prepares the study, who develops his own expertise as a result of writing the report, and
his colleagues, who use the study as a reference in their own
work.

Intelligence planners need to distinguish between the research undertaken by the analyst and the paper that goes out
of the office. The analyst must be allowed to do the research
necessary for a detailed understanding of his area of expertise, but there is usually little reason to put all of this research
into a formal study that, unfortunately or not, few people will
read. For example, a Soviet analyst should be encouraged to
study the upcoming generation of Soviet scientists in exquisite detail, but most reports the analyst provides a consumer
should focus on a specific question, such as what the political
views of a particular Soviet scientist are, or whether Soviet
scientists have a cadre of specialists in super-cooled microchip
technology.

In addition to orienting the intelligence product around
the needs of specific intelligence consumers (which many analytic agencies already do), the process for planning analysis
needs to be "consumer-oriented" as well. Intelligence managers already find themselves departing from the approved
annual production plan more and more in order to produce
the informal, quick-turnaround typescripts preferred by intelligence consumers. Indeed, the annual production plan
may itself be outliving its usefulness, and the ad hoc sched-
uling of typescripts may well be a better reflection of the true
requirements of intelligence consumers.

*4. The value of National Intelligence Estimates and other coordi-
nated interagency intelligence memoranda lies at least as much in the
exercise of producing the product as in the product itself.* As one
longtime intelligence analyst told the authors, no one has
ever won a high-level policy debate by waving an NIE in the
air and saying, "But this is what the Estimate says!" In truth,

an NIE, or, for that matter, any other coordinated intelligence product, simply reflects the "best truth" on which the community has settled at a given moment, with all the limitations of information and the idiosyncratic quirks that shaped its drafting and coordination.

Any estimate can err, but, if the coordination process works as it should, disagreements within the community will focus the attention of analysts on the specific questions that must be answered in order to resolve these differences. Over time, this process can improve the degree of certainty the community can claim for its estimates on a given subject.

Steps (most mentioned in earlier chapters, and many already being adopted in the community) that facilitate this self-correcting process include:

— allowing the development of various centers of opinion on intelligence issues within the intelligence community (bearing in mind the dangers of institutional biases that may develop within organizations);

— including dissents and their rationale in the main body of coordinated estimates;

— organizing research programs so that they include work that focuses on the pivotal issues identified in the dissents within coordinated estimates;

— indicating the degree of uncertainty associated with these pivotal issues in coordinated estimates, so that the consumer can consider the likely range of variation that the estimates could contain.

5. *Intelligence funding should be decoupled from fluctuations in defense spending.* The defense budget has probably been the single most significant factor in determining how much money the United States has spent on intelligence during the past forty years. This is disturbing because the outlook for higher levels of defense spending is not bright, and, if inflation-adjusted defense budgets ever again fall to the levels of the mid-1970s, and intelligence is tied to defense spending,

then real spending on intelligence could be cut anywhere from a quarter to a third. It is hard to imagine how the intelligence community could carry out even the most basic missions in such a situation.

More important, though, is that linking intelligence to defense vitiates the most carefully planned strategy for intelligence. It is simply impossible to make effective intelligence policy when, after intelligence planners make all of the complex trade-offs among collection systems and between alternative programs for analysis, the main factor determining intelligence policy is simply the total amount of money the United States happens to spend on defense.

To be sure, a one-fourth cut in intelligence spending is unlikely, if only because the intelligence community is better represented today in government councils: the stature of the DCI has been reinforced by executive orders; the intelligence committees are able to work in behalf of effective intelligence in Congress; a three-star flag officer heads DIA and is able to make a strong case in behalf of defense intelligence programs; and so on. However, democratic systems often behave in unpredictable and surprising ways, and it is possible that large reductions in intelligence could occur even if most officials and the public at large do not intend them to be made. Also, if intelligence spending remains firmly tied to defense spending, and if the defense budget is unlikely to grow much larger than it is today, then it would seem logical to conclude that it is also unlikely for the intelligence budget to be much bigger than it is today—even though the demands the intelligence community is expected to meet continue to grow and the cost of intelligence collection systems continues to rise.

To avert these potential problems, intelligence budgets must be decoupled from defense spending. Of course, we will always have to make choices between defense priorities and intelligence priorities, just as we make choices between defense and education, or education and health care. But decoupling intelligence from defense would ensure that attention is focused on intelligence issues when the intelligence budget is being decided and would help keep unrelated issues from arbitrarily deciding the outcome of such debates.

Decoupling the intelligence budget fully, while keeping it secret, would require:

— establishing a separate budget line to compensate the intelligence community when substantial reductions are being made in defense spending;

— assigning budget authority over this new line to the Director of Central Intelligence, without requiring the approval of the Secretary of Defense; and

— assigning jurisdiction over this new budget line in Congress to the Intelligence committees only, so that it is voted on separately from the Defense authorization.

6. National security policy initiatives such as arms control treaties, changes in military doctrine, and development of new weapons systems must be planned in a way that ensures that they will not require more intelligence support than will be available.

Intelligence consumers need to be accountable for the intelligence support they request. For example, sometimes the armed services develop and deploy weapons systems without considering the intelligence these weapons require. This creates problems. First, when intelligence officials do not know that a new weapon system will require special intelligence support (say, targeting data), they often fail to plan the additional analysts or technical systems necessary to provide this support. Second—and even more important—the armed services may deploy weapons that are simply beyond the capabilities of the intelligence community to support in operation.

This problem usually appears in weapons systems, but it is just as important in other areas of national security policy as well. Consider arms control, for instance. If intelligence requirements are not considered when an arms control proposal is first being formulated, a president may find to his unwelcome surprise that he is committed to an arms control proposal that cannot be monitored. If the administration negotiates the treaty anyway, the treaty may fail to receive approval from the Senate because a third of its members believe the treaty cannot be verified with sufficient confidence.

To avoid such surprises, at least two measures are necessary:

— requiring an "intelligence impact statement" for all major new weapon systems and foreign policy initiatives identifying the intelligence support the program will require;

— requiring inclusion of an "intelligence overhead" cost in the pricing of new weapon systems.

These steps are necessary not only to estimate intelligence requirements but also to guide the program itself, so that policy ambitions do not exceed intelligence capabilities. So, for instance, if U.S. officials develop a proposal for a global, comprehensive nuclear test ban treaty they would have to address the cost and feasibility of a global monitoring system capable of detecting violations.

As with most questions concerning intelligence, deciding how much intelligence is sufficient for monitoring an arms control treaty or supporting a weapon system would depend greatly on subjective factors. For instance, in the case of arms control, officials would have to decide how much risk of a violation would be acceptable. In the case of a weapon system, military officials would have to decide how much risk they could accept in being able to locate and hit a target. But requiring an impact statement would at least make the technical constraints and necessary expenditures explicit. Also, the requirement to attach intelligence funding to the program requiring the intelligence support would ensure that the problem would not "slip between the cracks." A program that depended on intelligence support to operate could not proceed faster than the intelligence resources were being provided.

7. Ambiguities about the responsibilities and prerogatives of intelligence officials and intelligence agencies invite trouble and must be clarified. In almost all forms of government, accountability is the incentive structure that promotes effectiveness. The executive orders, national security decision directives, legislative amendments, and congressional resolutions governing U.S. intelligence activities today, unfortunately, are too vague. In some cases they do not provide adequate executive or legislative oversight. In other cases they do not clearly assign responsibility. For example, some of the issues that the existing aggregation of regulations do not make clear include:

— when intelligence is required in specific kinds of national security decisions, and how this intelligence will be developed;

— the policy role—or, ideally, the lack of a policy role—of the Director of Central Intelligence as the principal intelligence advisor to the President and the National Security Council;

— the authority of officials outside the intelligence community to create requirements for intelligence resources;

— the process through which and conditions under which Congress should have access to intelligence data so that Congress can carry out its own national security responsibilities.

Following the congressional investigations of the intelligence community in the mid-1970s, these issues were to have been addressed by a comprehensive intelligence community charter. The push for a charter died during the Carter administration, largely over the degree of oversight the Congress should exercise over covert action. Unfortunately, when the conflict over covert action doomed the charter, the opportunity to settle issues such as how to ensure accountability for analysis, how to assign responsibility for intelligence production, and how to maintain security on a communitywide basis was also lost. Accountability and oversight of covert action, is, of course, a critical issue. The question of whether covert action is a proper policy option for the United States penetrates to the very center of the conflict between secrecy and American democracy. Yet it makes little sense to continue to avoid addressing the legal framework necessary for effective strategic intelligence because we cannot reach a consensus on covert action—especially when one considers how small a component covert action really is in the national intelligence program. A new legal framework governing intelligence activities will be essential to the survival of the intelligence community in a government that is increasingly open to debate and public scrutiny.

As we said at the beginning, planning, tradecraft, and organization are necessary but not sufficient conditions for successful strategic intelligence. These factors only define the limits of our capability. In the end, the effectiveness of intelligence depends on more than just the insight and skills of analysts, the dedication of case officers, the ingenuity of technicians, and the imagination of managers. The most important lesson of the past forty years is that successful intelligence requires capable people both to produce intelligence and to use it.

The Intelligence Cycle:
A Checklist of What Can Go Wrong

Accurate intelligence requires not only collecting and analyzing information but also avoiding certain types of errors that have consistently occurred in the production of strategic intelligence. One way of understanding these errors is to consider them as things that can go awry at each step in the intelligence cycle. In this appendix, we summarize the intelligence cycle, with particular emphasis on the tasks that must be completed at each step and the problems that can occur. These problems are illustrated with examples from past experiences and with citations from the text and other sources.

AN OUTLINE OF THE INTELLIGENCE
PROCESS AND POTENTIAL ERRORS

STEP I: Determining the Information Intelligence Consumers Require

A. Intelligence consumer presents a problem to the community, either by:

1. developing questions for analysis, or
2. requesting additional information on problems that the intelligence community brings to the attention of the consumer.

Potential Causes of Failure

— *Consumer does not provide the intelligence community adequate guidance.* Example: In the early 1970s, top U.S. officials were unaware both of the short-term Soviet agricultural difficulties and the impact the Soviet entry into the international grain market would have on U.S. interests. As a result, they failed to ask the intelligence community to give a high priority to collecting information on Soviet grain purchases.[1]

APPENDIX A

— *Consumer requests an answer to what is essentially a mystery (i.e., a question that logically or practically precludes a definitive answer).* Example: The requirement levied by U.S. officials during the 1970s for the intelligence community to estimate Soviet "global intentions" (Chap. 4, pp. 103–106).

B. Intelligence planners determine priorities for addressing the problem

Potential Causes of Failure

— *Intelligence officials assign the problem a low priority because they lack information sources or fear that addressing certain questions would undermine accepted policy.* Example: The reluctance of U.S. intelligence community to question the likelihood the Shah of Iran would retain power (Chap. 4, p. 107).

C. Requirements lists are prepared by ic Staff and circulated to agencies and policymakers

Potential Causes of Failure

— *Policymakers and intelligence officials fail to take the planning exercise seriously and respond perfunctorily to intelligence community's efforts to raise new questions.* Example: The cursory attention sometimes paid by officials to the DCI's efforts to develop "Key Intelligence Questions" and "National Intelligence Topics" during the 1970s (Chap. 2, pp. 46–49).

— *The interagency process lowers the priority of issues that later turn out to be important.* Example: The neglect of political and social events in Portugal in the early 1970s, leaving the United States ill-prepared for the Communist threat to Portugese democratization after the demise of the Salazar regime (Chap. 3, pp. 77–80).

STEP II: *Collection*

A. Community plans systems and collection strategy
   1. Collection planners identify and assess targets that will yield information to meet requirements.

2. Collection planners investigate and assess potential technologies and HUMINT methods for collecting data from the targets identified in preceding step.
3. The community conducts trade-off analysis among candidate collection methods to determine the best mix for meeting priorities.

Potential Causes of Failure

— *Analysts and other individuals with valid ideas for profitable targets are cut out of the planning process.* Example: The lack of attention prior to the mid-1970s to collecting information on the Soviet five-year planning process and its relationship to military deployments.[2]

— *Overreliance on existing or bureaucratically established collection sources rather than exploration of the possible payoffs from developing different collection approaches.* Example: Reliance on embassy and Savak (the Shah's secret police) reporting during the 1978/1979 Iranian revolution (Chap. 4, p. 108).

B. Community develops and deploys collection systems
   1. Community requests funding through executive branch and congressional budget reviews.
   2. Officials and contractors authorized to develop the system.

Potential Causes of Failure

— *Community does not request resources to collect data later proved to be required.* Examples: The situation in the earlier years of the Cold War, when Western intelligence services, which had been oriented toward Germany and Japan, had few agents or technical reconnaissance systems suitable for use against the new Soviet target (Chap. 3, pp. 64–66).[3] The relative neglect of U.S. collection capabilities (especially HUMINT capabilities) in Central America prior to the political crises in El Salvador and Nicaragua.[4]

— *Technological failures or delays.* Example: The reported early difficulties the U.S. intelligence community had in perfecting the film-recovery capsules from the initial photoreconnaissance satellites.[5]

— *Compromise of collection programs by lax security practices of government agencies or private contractors.* Examples: The loss of intelligence incurred by the the sale of SIGINT satellite information by contractor employees to Soviet intelligence in 1976; similar losses resulting from the compromise of an imaging system by a CIA employee in 1977 and the compromising of sensitive collection capabilities via an NSA employee in 1985.[6]

— *Technical failures.* Example: The loss of U.S. capabilities to place many types of reconnaissance satellites into orbit in 1985/1986 following the loss of the *Challenger* and failures of some expendable launch vehicles.[7]

C. Community initiates collection
  1. Collection targets are assigned priorities.
  2. Intelligence collection planners allocate the systems necessary to collect the required data and target them accordingly.
  3. Raw data is collected and processed into a form suitable for analysis.
  4. Data is disseminated in a timely fashion to appropriate analysts, while maintaining adequate compartmentation for security.

Potential Causes of Failure

— *Ad hoc restrictions on collection activities for threat or political reasons.* Examples: Restrictions placed on U-2 flights over the Soviet Union following the developments of SA-2 surface-to-air missiles by the Soviets; prohibitions placed on U-2 flights over Cuba during the height of the Missile Crisis; prohibitions of SR-71 flights over China during the 1971 Nixon-Mao summit.[8]

— *Interference from weather or other natural phenomena.* Examples: The reported difficulty the U.S. intelligence community had in tracking Soviet ICBM deployments with U-2 reconnaissance in 1959 and 1960 owing to cloud cover; later, the similar difficulties reported by the press of the U.S. intelligence community in pinpointing the Soviet phased array radar under construction at Krasnoyarsk in the early 1980s.[9]

A CHECKLIST OF WHAT CAN GO WRONG

— *Lack of adequate capacity to handle the flow of data effectively (i.e., system overload, lack of surge capacity).* Examples: The inability of NATO Headquarters to process and analyze the incoming intelligence information in the hours preceding the 1968 Soviet invasion of Czechoslovakia; the communication delays encountered by the NSA station that first had picked up intercepts of the Soviet shootdown of KAL 007 in September 1983.[10]

— *Lack of coordination and, hence, necessary synergism for tasks requiring multisource collection.* Example: Lack of coordination of SIGINT and imagery by RAF during efforts to locate and analyze German radar in World War II (Chap. 2, pp. 40–42).

— *Unwillingness of the community to modify routine collection procedures to meet ad hoc requirements.* Example: Inability of the community to meet the President's requests for specific imagery in the early days of the Carter administration (Chap. 6, pp. 162–163).

— *Denial of data, camouflage, concealment.* Example: Soviet efforts to hide the testing and exercising of their mobile land-based missiles (Chap. 3, pp. 76–77), and limiting such operations to nighttime.[11]

STEP III: Analysis and Coordination of Assessments Results

A. Analyst selects analytical technique, key assumptions, and data to be used, and carries out analysis.

Potential Causes of Failure

— *Analysts encounter methodological problems associated with validating or proving the assumptions underlying an assessment, including:*

  · *The equal plausibility of assumptions, neither of which can be proven superior on the basis of the available data.* Example: CIA and DIA differences during the mid-1970s over the range of the Backfire bomber, stemming from the differing assumptions underlying the analytic models each agency used (Chap. 4, pp. 93–94).

  · *Errors in the assumptions concerning the type of calculations made by an opponent.* Examples: U.S. and

Israeli estimates up to mid-1973 assumed that Egypt would not initiate a war against Israel in which it could not achieve military victory. Also, assumptions in NIE 11-3/8 during the 1960s to the effect that the Soviet Union's leaders would plan to deploy roughly the same number of ICBMs as the United States for the sake of stability (Chap. 4, pp. 91–93).[12]

- *Errors in the assumptions concerning an opponent's perception of the current situation.* Example: Estimates by the U.S. intelligence community in 1962 that Soviet leaders would view the introduction of nuclear weapons into Cuba as risky and highly threatening to the United States, and, hence, would not do so.[13]

— *Analysts fail to recognize the "signal-to-noise problem."* Examples: The failure to discern the indications of the impending Japanese attack on Pearl Harbor in the general flow of intelligence that was available (Chap. 5, pp. 111–112); the failure to detect preparations by North Korea to invade South Korea in 1950 (Chap. 1, pp. 4–5).

— *Analysts fall victim to problems associated with deception or disinformation, including:*

  - *False representation of plans or capabilities.* Examples: The inflated capabilities of the Soviet Strategic Rocket Forces claimed by Nikita Khrushchev prior to 1961 (Chap. 4, pp. 98–99); Germany's misrepresentation of the specifications of the battleship *Bismarck* in 1938 (Chap. 4, pp. 99–100).

  - *Forged documents, planted through various means.* Examples: Operation Mincemeat prior to the Allied invasion of Sicily; Allied deception of the true target of the D-Day invasion in 1944 (Chap. 4, p. 96).

  - *Misrepresentation of unconcealable activity.* Example: Soviet announcements prior to the invasion of Czechoslovakia that the Army was planning a Rear Services exercise.[14]

  - *"False negative" problem.* Example: Initial CIA rejection of Nosenko as *bona fide* defector on basis of prior failures to detect Philby and other penetrations (Chap. 4, pp. 101–102).

— *Analysts and collectors fall victim to errors in the processing, evaluation, or use of information, including*:

- *Limitation of data to familiar type.* Example: The tendency of CIA analysts to rely excessively on embassy reporting in developing their estimates of the international petroleum market prior to the 1973/1974 price surge (Chap. 2, p. 54).

- *Ignoring relevant data because no all-source centralized storage, retrieval, and distribution system exists.* Example: The failure by U.S. intelligence agencies in 1941 to correlate data that would have provided adequate indications and warning of the impending Japanese attack on Pearl Harbor (Chap. 5, p. 112).

- *Mistakenly eliminating valid evidence on the basis of suspicions that it is disinformation or inaccurate information provided for a vested interest.* Example: The discounting of emigré reports prior to October 1962 indicating that the Soviets were introducing offensive missiles into Cuba (Chap. 4, p. 101).

- *Mistaking newly collected information for an entirely new situation or development.* Example: NSA and CIA reports in 1979 erroneously identifying a Soviet unit that had been in Cuba since the early 1960s for a new Soviet "combat brigade" (Chap. 4, p. 102).

B. Office/agency/community reviews and coordinates analysis
  1. Coordination: relevant other offices and agencies respond to draft intelligence assessment; range of views are identified; differences in underlying assumptions and interpretation of data are identified, resolved (if possible), or highlighted (if not).
  2. Evaluation of product for accuracy, referral of any issues in dispute to intelligence planners to develop decisive tests or collection of data necessary to resolve ambiguity.

Potential Causes of Failure
— *Errors are produced in an estimate as a result of institutional biases including*:

- *Institutional reluctance to depart from previous estimates and theories.* Examples: The insistence by CIA analysts that the political situation in Iran in 1978 was not in even a "prerevolutionary" state and that the Shah would deal with his opponents as well as he did in prior instances; reluctance of Air Force intelligence to abandon prior estimates of Soviet ICBM deployments even after clear imagery evidence to the contrary (Chap. 4, pp. 98–99).

- "Groupthink" or reduction of intelligence to the "lowest common denominator" or opinion. Example: The consensus achieved within the intelligence community over the likelihood of success of Operation Zapata (Bay of Pigs invasion) and the unlikelihood that Soviet missiles would be deployed in Cuba.[15]

- Policy-induced bias. Example: The underestimation by most intelligence community analysts of the scope and seriousness of political and religious opposition to the Shah in 1979 (Chap. 4, pp. 107–108).

- Selection of incorrect estimate by coordination. Example: Soviet ICBM estimates, 1957–1960, which essentially averaged differences in agency judgments rather than resolved or explained them (Chap. 5, pp. 125–130).

- Errors in existing assessments are not corrected because of a lack of adequate monitoring of intelligence product and follow-up to rectify errors. Example: The lack of prompt response to the intelligence community's underestimates of Soviet strategic forces during the 1960s (Chap. 5, p. 136).

STEP IV: *Dissemination of the Product*

Potential Causes of Failure

- Dissemination of the intelligence product is delayed, is inefficient, or is in an ineffective medium for the consumer. Example: Failure of the NFIB to issue the 1978 National Intelligence Estimate on the political situation in Iran prior to the unrest that eventually unseated the Shah, which forced policymakers to rely on uncoordinated drafts or single agency viewpoint and current reporting.[16]

APPENDIX B

Glossary

BNE	Board of National Estimates: a panel of senior analysts responsible for overseeing the production of National Intelligence Estimates until it was disbanded in 1974.
CC&D	Camouflage, concealment, and deception measures.
CIG	Central Intelligence Group: the post-World War II predecessor of the CIA.
CODEWORD	A designator assigned to a category of intelligence in order to limit its dissemination.
COMINT	"Communications intelligence": information obtained by the intercept and analysis of opponents' transmitted messages over open airwaves, cables, and other media; a subset of SIGINT.
COMIREX	Committee on Imagery Requirements and Exploitation: a body of representatives from various intelligence agencies assigned responsibility for coordinating collection by current national imagery systems and planning of future systems; housed within the IC Staff.
COMOR	Committee on Overhead Reconnaissance: predecessor of COMIREX.
COMPARTMENTATION	The practice of dividing intelligence data into categories and limiting access to each on a "need to know" basis; objective is to minimize losses if security measures fail.
CPSU	Communist Party of the Soviet Union.
DCI	Director of Central Intelligence.

DCID 1/2	Literally "Director of Central Intelligence Directive": a comprehensive list of countries and subjects, indicating the priority of each for intelligence collection; intended as a management tool for the intelligence community.
DDI	Deputy Director for Intelligence: official responsible for most CIA analytic units; also refers to the Directorate of Intelligence, which the DDI manages.
DDO	Deputy Director for Operations: official responsible for CIA human collection and covert action; also refers to the Directorate of Operations, which the DDO manages.
DDS&T	Deputy Director for Science and Technology: official responsible for certain CIA scientific and technical analytic units and for the planning and operation of certain CIA technical collection systems; also refers to the Directorate of Science and Technology, which the DDS&T manages.
DIA	Defense Intelligence Agency.
DIE	Defense Intelligence Estimate: an intelligence analysis coordinated among Defense Department intelligence units (DIA, Air Force Intelligence, Office of Naval Intelligence, etc.).
DOD	Department of Defense.
ELINT	"Electronic intelligence": information derived from the collection and analysis of opponents' radar and other electromagnetic emissions not containing messages; a subset of SIGINT.
ELV	"Expendable launch vehicle": a rocket booster used to place satellites into orbit.
GDIP	General Defense Intelligence Program: the administrative umbrella under which all Defense Department intelligence programs serving a national audience are organized.

GRU	Soviet military intelligence agency (from Russian acronym for "Main Intelligence Directorate").
HAC	House Appropriations Committee.
HASC	House Armed Services Committee
HUMINT	Intelligence data collected via human sources.
IA	Imagery analyst.
ICBM	Intercontinental ballistic missile.
IC Staff	Intelligence Community Staff: a secretariat established to support the Director of Central Intelligence in his assignments as head of the national intelligence community.
INR	Bureau of Intelligence and Research: State Department component responsible for intelligence analysis and contributing to community estimates.
IRBM	Intermediate-range ballistic missile.
KGB	Soviet intelligence service (from Russian acronym for "Committee for State Security").
KIQS	Key Intelligence Questions: a set of issues of critical interest to the intelligence community, developed by William Colby while DCI as a management aid (see also NITs).
LANDSAT	A U.S. civilian earth survey and imagery satellite.
MAGIC	Codeword used by the U.S. in World War II to designate deciphered signals intelligence collected from Japanese sources.
MI	Military Intelligence: term used to refer to U.S. Army intelligence units, mainly through the end of World War II and the establishment of the modern intelligence community.
NFAC	National Foreign Assessment Center: the name assigned to the DDI from 1977 to 1981

(the DDI was himself referred to as the
D/NFAC).

NFIB   National Foreign Intelligence Board: a
panel consisting of the principals of the analytic agencies of the intelligence community
(e.g., CIA, INR, DIA, etc.); acts as a "board of
directors" responsible for the production of
NIEs and other interagency estimates.

NFIP   National Foreign Intelligence Program: the
combined programs of CIA, INR, GDIP, NSA,
and other agencies responsible for national
intelligence; managed by the Director of
Central Intelligence.

NIC   National Intelligence Council: the body en-
compassing the NIOs and responsible for the
development of NIEs.

NID   National Intelligence Daily: an intelligence
publication produced by the CIA.

NIE   National Intelligence Estimate: a series of
comprehensive, coordinated, interagency
intelligence assessments on designated subjects, e.g., NIE 11–3/8–86 is the NIE prepared
in 1986 on Soviet strategic forces.

NIO   National Intelligence Officer: a senior analyst assigned primary responsibility for covering a topic or geographical region of intelligence interest, e.g., the NIO/CT is
responsible for intelligence on counterter-
rorism.

NIS   National Intelligence Survey: a series of
briefs on foreign countries; originally published by the CIA after World War II, currently published outside the intelligence
community.

NITS   National Intelligence Topics: a list of subjects of primary concern to the intelligence
community, developed by Stansfield Turner
while DCI as a system for planning intelli-

gence; successor to Key Intelligence Questions (KIQs).

NSA	National Security Agency: primary organization for collecting and processing signals intelligence.
NSC	National Security Council.
OCI	Office of Current Intelligence: a CIA component responsible for producing intelligence periodicals, eventually subsumed into the DDI.
OMB	Office of Management and Budget.
ONE	Office of National Estimates: a component housed within the CIA until the mid-1970s; responsible for supporting the Board of National Estimates in the preparation of NIEs.
ONI	Office of Naval Intelligence.
ORE	Office of Research and Evaluation.
ORR	Office of Research and Reports: a CIA analytical component eventually subsumed into the DDI.
OSD	Office of the Secretary of Defense.
OSI	Office of Scientific Intelligence: a CIA component eventually subsumed into the DDS&T.
OSS	Office of Strategic Services: a World War II intelligence service commonly accepted as the predecessor of the CIA.
PDB	*President's Daily Brief*: a highly classified, limited distribution intelligence publication produced by the CIA for the President and designated NSC officials.
PI	"Photo Interpreter": currently often referred to as an "IA," or "Imagery Analyst."
PR units	"Photo Reconnaissance": components attached to various RAF operational units during World War II.

RADINT	"Radar intelligence": intelligence derived by scanning opposition targets with radar (also see ELINT).
RAF	Royal Air Force.
SAC	Strategic Air Command (U.S. Air Force).
SCI	Special Compartmented Information: a system of restricting the circulation of specified categories of intelligence by classifying this information within a system of "codewords."
SIGINT	"Signals intelligence": includes COMINT, RADINT, ELINT, etc.
SIS	Secret Intelligence Service: a British intelligence organization.
SLBM	Submarine-launched ballistic missile.
SLU	Special Liaison Units: mobile teams assigned by the British to their operational military units in the field to distribute ULTRA intelligence and maintain security over signals intelligence.
SPOT	A French civilian earth reconnaissance satellite; abbreviated from "*System Probatoire d'Observation de la Terre.*"
SRF	Strategic Rocket Forces: Soviet military service responsible for long-range missiles.
SR-71	High altitude, high-speed reconnaissance aircraft developed by the CIA as a successor to the U–2; currently operated by the Air Force.
TIARA	"Tactical Intelligence and Related Activities": the collected set of Defense Department intelligence programs intended primarily to provide operational intelligence to U.S. military units; managed by the Assistant Secretary of Defense for Command, Control, Communications, and Intelligence.
ULTRA	Codeword used by Great Britain (and, later, the United States) to designate deciphered

signals intelligence collected from German sources.

USCIB   U.S. Communications Intelligence Board: a Defense Department body established for a short period after World War II, responsible for coordinating the collection of signals intelligence by the military services.

USIB   U.S. Intelligence Board: predecessor of NFIB.

U-2   A high-altitude reconnaissance aircraft developed by the CIA in the early 1950s, currently operated by the Air Force.

Y Service   Component of RAF responsible for the interception and initial processing of signals intelligence during World War II.

APPENDIX C

List of Officials Interviewed

The individuals interviewed for this study held the following positions in government. The numbers in parentheses indicate when more than one person holding a particular position was interviewed (e.g., three Directors of Central Intelligence were interviewed). Participants who spoke of their experiences from the perspective of two different offices are listed for each of these positions. A total of sixty individuals were interviewed.

Central Intelligence Agency
Director of Central Intelligence (3)
Deputy Director of Central Intelligence (2)
Chairman, National Intelligence Council
National Intelligence Officer for the USSR (6)
Deputy Director for Intelligence (3)
Deputy Director for Science and Technology
Director, Office of National Estimates
Director, Office of Scientific Intelligence
Director, Office of Weapons Intelligence
Director, Office of Training and Education (3)
Senior Analyst (5)
Analyst (4)

Department of Defense
Assistant Secretary of Defense for Intelligence
Director, Defense Intelligence Agency (3)
Director, National Security Agency
Assistant Chief of Staff, Air Force Intelligence (3)
Assistant Chief of Staff, Army Intelligence
Director, Office of Naval Intelligence
Deputy Director for Estimates, Defense Intelligence Agency
Analyst, Defense Intelligence Agency (4)

LIST OF OFFICIALS INTERVIEWED

Department of State
Assistant Secretary of State/Director, Bureau of Intelligence and Research (2)
Analyst, Bureau for Intelligence and Research (4)

National Security Council
Assistant to the President for National Security (3)
Senior Staff Member (6)
Staff Member (3)

Intelligence Community Staff
Staff Member (4)

Notes

CHAPTER ONE

1. Sherman Kent, *Strategic Intelligence for American World Policy* (Princeton, N.J.: Princeton University Press, 1949).

2. See, for example, Rose Mary Sheldon, "Toga and Dagger," *Washington Post* July 16, 1985, p. A15; Sheldon, "The Roman Secret Service," *Intelligence Quarterly* (July 1985), pp. 1–2; Sheldon, "Hannibal's Spies," *International Journal of Intelligence and Counterintelligence* 1, no. 3 (Fall, 1986): 53–70; and Francis Dvornic, *Origins of Intelligence Services* (New Brunswick, N.J.: Rutgers University Press, 1974).

3. Harold P. Ford, "A Tribute to Sherman Kent," *Studies in Intelligence* (Fall 1980), p. 4. *Studies* is a CIA professional journal that contains classified as well as unclassified articles. The latter can be obtained by writing to the Agency's office of public affairs.

4. See U.S., Congress, Senate, 94th Cong., 2d sess., *Final Report of the Select Committee to Study Governmental Operations with Respect to Intelligence Activities* (Washington, D.C.: U.S. Government Printing Office, April 1976), 6: 66–74 (hereafter the *Church Committee Report*).

5. See Herbert O. Yardley, *The American Black Chamber* (Indianapolis: Bobbs-Merrill, 1931); and David Kahn, *The Codebreakers* (New York: Macmillan, 1967), chap. 12.

6. Bradley F. Smith, *The Shadow Warriors: OSS and the Origins of the CIA* (New York: Basic Books, 1983), pp. 360–389; and *Church Committee Report* 6: 137–156.

7. Anthony Cave Brown, *The Last Hero: Wild Bill Donovan* (New York: Times Books, 1982), pp. 619–633; Thomas F. Troy, *Donovan and the CIA* (Washington, D.C.: Central Intelligence Agency, 1981), pp. 217–229, 287–304.

8. *Church Committee Report* 1: 100.

9. A current version and legislative history of the National Security Act of 1947 pertaining to intelligence matters is to be found in U.S., Congress, House, Permanent Select Committee on Intelli-

gence, *A Compilation of Intelligence Laws and Related Laws and Executive Orders of Interest to the National Intelligence Community* (Washington, D.C.: U.S. Government Printing Office, July 1985), pp. 3–20.

10. These developments in the CIA structure are chronicled in Ray S. Cline, *The CIA under Reagan, Bush, and Casey* (Washington, D.C.: Acropolis Books, 1981).

11. Since the creation of the DIA, its critics have claimed that its estimates merely parrot the Defense Department's line; some have criticized the quality of DIA estimates themselves.

Former DCI Stansfield Turner, one of these critics, claims that DIA is unable to resist the pulls and pressures of the military services and, at least during his tenure, lacked quality management; see his *Secrecy and Democracy: The CIA in Transition* (New York: Houghton Mifflin, 1985), pp. 246–247. Indeed, former DIA directors have themselves cited efforts they made to improve analysis within DIA, implying a need for improvement during the early years of the organization's existence.

A fairer assessment, however, seems to be that DIA has directed its greatest efforts in the particular areas in which its customers make the greatest demands, such as support for military operations, target planning, and so on. These activities have much less visibility than does, say, DIA's participation in NIEs or the political intelligence summaries it provides for military officials, which may account for the popular perception of DIA. On the other hand, there clearly is a strategic intelligence component in many operational intelligence decisions; target planning, for example, depends greatly on an assessment of which targets are likely to have the greatest effect on the overall capabilities of an opponent.

12. Albert Wohlstetter, "Is There a Strategic Arms Race?" *Foreign Policy*, no. 15 (Summer 1974); "Rivals But No Race," *Foreign Policy* no. 16 (Fall 1974); and "Legends of the Strategic Arms Race," USSI Report 75–1 (Washington, D.C.: United States Strategic Institute, 1975).

13. Ray S. Cline, "Policy without Intelligence," *Foreign Policy*, no. 17 (Winter 1974), pp. 121–135.

14. William Colby, *Honorable Men* (New York: Simon and Schuster, 1978), pp. 352–360.

15. See Zbigniew Brzezinski, *Power and Principle* (New York: Farrar, Straus, Giroux, 1983), pp. 395–396.

16. Philip Taubman, "Casey and His CIA on the Rebound," *New York Times Magazine*, January 16, 1983, p. 35.

17. See, for example, Steven Engleberg's article in the *New York Times*, August 31, 1987, p. A1; for a rebuttal, see Henry S. Rowen's letter to the editor of September 13, 1987.

18. *Church Committee Report* 4: 19.

19. For example, during the 1970s, the CIA undertook a greater role monitoring the international grain market, partly to serve as a double check on the Agriculture Department's estimates and partly in response to the lack of warning the United States had to the Soviet Union's massive grain purchases in the early 1970s. See Dan Morgan, *Merchants of Grain* (New York: Viking Press, 1979), pp. 50–51.

20. U.S., Senate, Committee on Armed Services, *Soviet Treaty Violations* (Washington, D.C.: U.S. Government Printing Office, 1984), pp. 10, 41.

21. See David Harper, *Official Secrets: The Use and Abuse of the Act* (London: Secker and Warburg, 1987).

22. Leading U.S. officials appear to understand the nuances of the game, and they play accordingly. In 1984, for example, many administration officials were openly arguing for "covert" aid to anti-Sandinista rebels in Nicaragua—an argument that would seem a contradiction in terms. Similarly, in 1986, Secretary of State George Shultz publicly argued for "covert" action to unseat Libyan leader Muammar Khaddafi to prove the determination of the United States to stop terrorism. See Bernard Gwertzman, "Shultz Advocates U.S. Covert Action Programs to Depose Qaddafi," *New York Times*, April 28, 1986, p. A7.

CHAPTER TWO

1. See Stansfield Turner's foreword to David D. Newsom, *The Soviet Brigade in Cuba: A Study in Political Diplomacy* (Bloomington, Ind.: Indiana University Press, 1987).

2. For an overview of the various analytical components within the intelligence community, see Jeffrey T. Richelson, *The U.S. Intelligence Community* (Cambridge, Mass.: Ballinger Publishing Company, 1985), chaps. 3–6.

3. See Andrew J. Brookes, *Photo Reconnaissance* (London: Ian Allan, Ltd., 1975), pp. 74–108; and Dino A. Brugioni, "Naval Photo Intel in WWII," *U.S. Naval Institute Proceedings* 113, no. 6 (June 1987): 46–51.

4. See Aileen Clayton, *The Enemy is Listening* (London: Hutchinson and Company, 1980).

5. See R. V. Jones, *The Secret War: British Scientific Intelligence, 1939–1945* (New York: Coward, McCann, and Geoghegan, 1978), pp. 189–202.

6. Jones, *The Secret War*, pp. 332–346.

7. William Colby, *Honorable Men* (New York: Simon and Schuster, 1978), pp. 330–331; also see *Church Committee Report* 1: 88–89.

8. *Church Committee Report* 4: 310–311.

9. Stansfield Turner, *Secrecy and Democracy: The CIA in Transition* (New York: Houghton Mifflin, 1985), pp. 18–19.

10. Scott D. Breckinridge, *The CIA and the U.S. Intelligence System* (Boulder, Colo.: Westview Press, 1986), p. 56.

11. See Colby, *Honorable Men*, p. 361; Breckinridge, *The CIA and the U.S. Intelligence System*, p. 61; Turner, *Secrecy and Democracy*, pp. 260–262.

12. The process for the Intelligence Capabilities Plan was described in generic terms by intelligence officials and former officials in interviews with the authors in 1984. The title of the plan was indicated in Bob Woodward, *Veil: The Secret Wars of the CIA, 1981–1987* (New York: Simon and Schuster, 1987), p. 179.

13. *Church Committee Report*, Book 1, p. 84.

14. See Ronald Lewin, *The American Magic: Codes, Ciphers, and the Defeat of Japan* (New York: Farrar, Straus, Giroux, 1982), pp. 118–122; and *Church Committee Report*, Book 1, p. 85.

15. *Church Committee Report*, Book 1, pp. 84–85.

16. James R. Killian, Jr., *Sputnik, Scientists, and Eisenhower* (Cambridge, Mass.: MIT Press, 1977), pp. 83–84.

17. Ray S. Cline, *The CIA under Reagan, Bush, and Casey* (Washington, D.C.: Acropolis Books, 1981), pp. 178–181.

18. Clayton, *The Enemy is Listening*, p. 125.

19. See, for example, Peter Calvocoressi, *Top Secret Ultra* (New York: Ballantine, 1980), pp. 63–65; and Nigel West, *MI-6: British Secret Intelligence Service Operations, 1909–1945* (New York: Random House, 1983), pp. 107–108.

20. See, for example, the findings of the Senate Select Committee on Intelligence, *U.S. Intelligence Analysis and the Oil Issue, 1973–1974* (Washington, D.C.: U.S. Government Printing Office, 1977), pp. 3–4.

21. David C. Martin, *Wilderness of Mirrors* (New York: Harper and Row, 1980), pp. 76–92.

22. For Cyrus Vance's description of the Iranian SIGINT operations and their role in verifying SALT, see his *Hard Choices* (New York: Harper and Row, 1983), p. 136; also see Strobe Talbott, *Endgame* (New York: Harper and Row, 1979), p. 252. For a description of the mission of the *Glomar Explorer* and the security and diplomatic challenges it presented, see Colby, *Honorable Men*, pp. 413–418.

23. *Church Committee Report*, Book 1, pp. 276–277.

24. Bradley F. Smith, *The Shadow Warriors: OSS and the Origins of the CIA* (New York: Basic Books, 1983), p. 263.

25. See, for example, Warren J. Keegan, "Multinational Scanning: A Study of the Information Sources Utilized by Headquarters Executives in Multinational Companies," *Administrative Science Quarterly* 19, no. 3 (September 1974): 411–421; Dolph Warren Zink, *The Political Risks for Multinational Enterprises in Developing Countries* (New York: Praeger, 1973); and T. H. Moran, ed., *International Political Risk Assessment: The State of the Art* (Washington, D.C.: Landegger Papers on International Business Diplomacy, 1987).

26. F. W. Winterbotham, *The Ultra Secret* (New York: Harper and Row, 1974), p. 21.

27. Sherman Kent, *Strategic Intelligence for American World Policy* (Princeton, N.J.: Princeton University Press, 1949), pp. 195–201.

28. Testimony of John Huizenga, *Church Committee Report*, Book 1, pp. 266–267. Though Kent was in favor of separating the intelligence and policymaking functions, he was also well aware of the possible costs; for example, see Kent, *Strategic Intelligence*, pp. 81–82.

CHAPTER THREE

1. For the development and use of the bombe, see F. W. Winterbotham, *The Ultra Secret* (New York: Harper and Row, 1974), pp. 15–16; and Ronald Lewin, *Ultra Goes to War* (London: Hutchinson and Company, 1978), pp. 41–42. For the development of direction finding and airborne receivers, see Aileen Clayton, *The Enemy is Listening* (London: Hutchinson and Company, 1980), pp. 65, 125. For the use of ELINT in scientific and technical analysis, see R. V. Jones, *The Wizard War: British Scientific Intelligence, 1939–1945* (New York: Coward, McCann & Geoghegan, 1978), pp. 190–286. For a portrayal of the events leading to British-American cooperation in intelligence, see William Stevenson, *A Man Called Intrepid* (New York:

Harcourt, Brace, Jovanovich, 1976), especially chap. 19. For the use and importance of traffic analysis in World War II SIGINT operations, see Ronald Lewin, *The American Magic: Codes, Ciphers, and the Defeat of Japan* (New York: Farrar, Straus, Giroux, 1982), pp. 89–90, 160–161; and Edwin T. Layton, *And I Was There* (New York: William Morrow, 1985), pp. 357–360.

2. Bradley F. Smith, *The Shadow Warriors: OSS and the Origins of the CIA* (New York: Basic Books, 1983), pp. 200–226.

3. For a discussion of the use of German and emigré intelligence assets, see John Prados, *Presidents' Secret Wars* (New York: William Morrow, 1986), pp. 36–37.

Over the years more and more details of U.S. human sources have either been declassified or leaked and subsequently authenticated; a recent depiction of the state of U.S. HUMINT sources at the onset of the Cold War appears in William Stevenson, *Intrepid's Last Case* (New York: Ballentine, 1983). For a portrayal of the contribution that embassy reporting made to assessments of the Soviet Union, see Daniel Yergin, *Shattered Peace: The Origins of the Cold War and the National Security State* (Boston: Little, Brown, 1977).

4. See Francis Gary Powers, *Operation Overflight* (New York: Holt, Rinehart, and Winston, 1970), pp. 7–8.

5. See U.S., Congress, Office of Technology Assessment, *Anti-Satellite Weapons, Countermeasures, and Arms Control* (Washington, D.C.: U.S. Government Printing Office, 1985), pp. 33–39.

Stansfield Turner describes Project Pyramider as a "system to provide a means for communicating with CIA agents, foreign agents, emplaced sensors, and [to] provide backup communications for overseas facilities." See his citation of CIA official Leslie C. Dirks' testimony at the Christopher Boyce espionage trial; see his *Secrecy and Democracy: The CIA in Transition* (New York: Houghton Mifflin, 1985), p. 64.

6. A scholarly overview of the development of the U.S. intelligence satellite program is given in Paul B. Stares, *The Militarization of Space, 1945–1984* (Ithaca, N.Y.: Cornell University Press, 1985), pp. 30–35.

7. See Powers, *Operation Overflight*, pp. 21–22. For an account of the British mission to photograph Kapustin Yar, see Joseph E. O'Connor, "Oral History Interview with Robert Amory, Jr." John F. Kennedy Library, February 9, 1966, pp. 112–113.

Using bombers, at least at that time, was not as unreasonable as it might seem today; in the late 1940s and early 1950s jet bombers could fly almost as fast as fighter interceptors and usually flew at higher altitudes; an interceptor needed good ground control support to catch a single bomber approaching from an unpredictable direction.

8. Jay Miller has written what are probably the most complete publicly available histories of the U-2 and SR-71 programs; see his *Lockheed U-2* (Austin, Tex.: Aerofax, 1983), and *Lockheed SR-72 (A-12/YF-12/D-21)* (Arlington, Tex.: Aerofax, 1985).

For an explanation of RC-135 missions flown to monitor Soviet missile tests, see Alexander Dallin, *Black Box: KAL 007 and the Superpowers* (Berkeley, Calif.: University of California Press, 1985); Seymour Hersh, *The Target is Destroyed* (New York: Vantage Press, 1986); and Philip Taubman, "U.S. Says Intelligence Plane Was on a Routine Mission," *New York Times*, September 5, 1983, p. 4.

9. See William Colby, *Honorable Men* (New York: Simon and Schuster, 1978), pp. 413–418.

10. For a discussion of the Iranian SIGINT sites, see Cyrus Vance, *Hard Choices* (New York: Harper and Row, 1983), p. 136.

11. For the Berlin Tunnel, see David C. Martin, *Wilderness of Mirrors* (New York: Harper and Row, 1980), pp. 76–92; the Clandestine Services History paper, *The Berlin Tunnel Operation* (Washington, D.C.: Central Intelligence Agency, 1967); and John Ranelagh, *The Agency: The Rise and Decline of the CIA* (New York: Simon and Schuster, 1986), pp. 289–290. For the Iranian SIGINT sites and the COBRA DANE radar on Shemya Island, see SALT II Agreement, Document No. 12B (Washington, D.C.: Department of State, 1979), pp. 43–45. For the mission to survey landing sites prior to the Iranian rescue mission, see Stansfield Turner's op ed piece in the *Washington Post*, November 23, 1985, p. E1.

12. For an overview of the capabilities and costs of LANDSAT (and its French competitor, SPOT), see Laurie McGinley, "Satellites May Give Journalists Powerful Tool," *Wall Street Journal*, July 2, 1986, p. 58. For an analysis of the various film and radar imaging experiments carried out on the space shuttle, see "Shuttle Instruments Providing Unprecedented Topographic Details," *Aviation Week and Space Technology* (April 8, 1985), pp. 49–51.

13. A good summary of the development of early ELINT operations appears in R. V. Jones, *The Wizard War*, chap. 23.

14. *Church Committee Report*, Book 1, p. 354.

15. Herbert Scoville, Jr., "Verification of Soviet Strategic Missile Tests," in William C. Potter, ed., *Verification and SALT: The Challenge*

of Strategic Deception (Boulder, Colo.: Westview Press, 1980), p. 167. Some indication of COBRA DANE's capability to analyze flying vehicles is indicated by the system's often-cited ability to detect "basketball-sized" objects.

16. See, for example, *Recent False Alerts from the Nation's Missile Attack Warning System*, U.S., Congress, Senate, Committee on Armed Services, 96th Cong., 2d sess. (Washington, D.C.: U.S. Government Printing Office, 1980); and Caspar W. Weinberger, *Annual Report to the Congress, Fiscal Year 1987* (Washington, D.C.: U.S. Department of Defense, 1986), p. 223.

17. James Shepley and Clay Blair, Jr., *The Hydrogen Bomb: The Men, The Menace, The Mechanism* (New York: David McKay Company, 1954), pp. 3–5. For a discussion of the analysis of nuclear debris, see Scoville, "Verification of Soviet Strategic Missile Tests," p. 163.

The original Vela system is no longer operational. The current satellite base for detecting nuclear explosions, which is installed on new Navstar Global Positioning System satellites, is described in Weinberger, *Annual Report to the Congress, Fiscal Year 1987*, p. 224.

The characteristic signature of a nuclear explosion is created by the temporary obscuring of the fireball by superheated gasses, which are opaque. In a nuclear explosion, thermal radiation is initially released by the detonation; then superheated gasses expand outward, trapping emitted light; and, finally, the fireball reappears when the gasses have cooled enough for light waves to escape again. This chain of events (all of which occurs in a fraction of a second) produces a unique "double flash" effect. See Kosta Tsipis, *Arsenal: Understanding Weapons in the Nuclear Age* (New York: Simon and Schuster, 1983), p. 41.

18. John Barron, *KGB Today: The Hidden Hand* (New York: Reader's Digest Press, 1983), pp. 269, 299.

19. Ray S. Cline, *The CIA under Reagan, Bush, and Casey* (Washington, D.C.: Acropolis Books, 1981), p. 270.

20. William J. Broad, "Civilians Use Satellite Photos for Spying on Soviet Military," *New York Times*, April 7, 1986, p. 1. The price for a SPOT photograph is $155 to $1,790, depending on the quality and resolution desired; given the capability of civilian imaging systems, only the highest-resolution imagery is likely to have intelligence value.

21. Viktor Suvorov, *Inside the Soviet Army* (New York: Macmillan, 1983), p. 106.

NOTES TO PAGES 78–83

22. U.S., Congress, Office of Technology Assessment, *Anti-Satellite Weapons, Countermeasures and Arms Control*, pp. 76–84. In addition, OTA studied active countermeasures (e.g., satellites that "shoot back" at attackers) and diplomatic measures (e.g., an ASAT ban). OTA also noted that a combination of measures could be used.

23. Charles Mohr, "Pentagon Fears Delays on Future Spy Satellites," *New York Times*, February 24, 1986, p. B6.

24. Scott D. Breckinridge, *CIA and the U.S. Intelligence System* (Boulder, Colo.: Westview Press, 1986), p. 130.

25. By necessity, these costs are only approximations used for the sake of illustration. Figures appearing in the federal budget for a satellite system give only total program costs, sometimes broken down into new investment, operations and maintenance, etc.; rarely does one find a "per satellite" cost.

LANDSAT D and LANDSAT D'—the first satellites in the series to use an electro-optical thematic mapper system—cost about $250 million per satellite in early-1980s dollars, but the system has several features that reduce its costs considerably in comparison with an intelligence satellite, e.g., LANDSAT uses a relatively simple stabilization system to keep the spacecraft's sensors oriented toward earth and is considerably less accurate than what would be required for intelligence-quality resolution. Even so, one can assume LANDSAT costs are within an order of magnitude of an intelligence imaging satellite, as the basic technology is similar. See U.S., Congress, House, Committee on Science and Technology, *Commercialization of Land and Weather Satellites* (Washington, D.C.: U.S. Government Printing Office, 1983), p. 37; Patricia E. Humphlett, *LANDSAT (Land Remote Sensing Satellite System)*, Issue Brief IB 82066 (Washington, D.C.: Congressional Research Service, December 1985).

26. See Jacques S. Gansler, *The Defense Industry* (Cambridge, Mass.: MIT Press, 1980), chap. 1.

27. For a similar view, see the comments of then-Deputy Assistant Secretary of Defense Frank J. Gaffney, cited in Walter Andrews, "U.S. Policy on Spy Satellites Risky, Pentagon Official Says," *Washington Times*, May 14, 1986, p. 4.

The private sector would, of course, continue to supply ideas that could be applied to intelligence, but this would be more true for basic research; the loss of experienced intelligence contractors would mostly be felt in a loss in the ability of industry to respond to the more practical aspects of intelligence technology.

28. For two views on the cost versus capability debate, see James

Fallows, *National Defense* (New York: Random House, 1981), chap. 3; and William Perry, "Fallows' Fallacies: A Review Essay," *International Security* 6, no. 4 (Spring 1982): 174–182.

29. See Bruce D. Berkowitz, "Technological Progress, Strategic Weapons, and American Nuclear Policy," *Orbis* 29, no. 2 (Summer 1985): 241–258.

30. See Bruce D. Berkowitz, "A New Role for Intelligence in Arms Control," *Studies in Intelligence* (Spring 1985), pp. 105–110.

CHAPTER FOUR

1. Sherman Kent, *Strategic Intelligence for American World Policy* (Princeton, N.J.: Princeton University Press, 1949), p. 10.

2. As Klaus Knorr observed, "Any problem-solving organization will evolve premises, analytical procedures, rules of thumb, and other intellectual practices that are based implicitly, if not explicitly, on hypotheses about the reality and about the kinds of events and consequences they must cope with. Such theory is informal rather than formal, apt to be fragmentary rather than integrated, the cumulative sediment of experience rather than the product of self-conscious endeavor." See his "Failures in National Intelligence Estimates: The Case of the Cuban Missiles," *World Politics* 16, no. 3 (April 1964): 4–66.

3. Ray S. Cline, *The CIA under Reagan, Bush, and Casey* (Washington, D.C.: Acropolis Books, 1981), p. 187.

4. Robert M. Gates and Lawrence K. Gershwin, *Soviet Strategic Force Developments*, testimony presented to Joint Session of the Subcommittee on Soviet and Theater Nuclear Forces, Senate Armed Services Committee and Defense Subcommittee of the Senate Committee on Appropriations (Washington, D.C.: Central Intelligence Agency, June 16, 1985).

5. For one example of the argument holding that U.S. deployments and arms control would significantly affect Soviet military deployments, see Secretary of Defense Harold Brown's testimony to the U.S. Senate on the SALT II agreement, printed in U.S. Department of State, *Current Policy* (July 9–11, 1979), no. 72A; for an example of the argument stating that the Five-Year Plan constrained Soviet responses, see David S. Sullivan, "Evaluating U.S. Intelligence Estimates," in Roy Godson, ed., *Intelligence Requirements for the 1980s: Analysis and Estimates* (New Brunswick, N.J.: Transaction Books, 1980), p. 63.

6. For a discussion of the various theories that could be used to analyze this kind of situation, see Graham T. Allison, *Essence of Decision* (Boston: Little, Brown, 1971).

7. Bruce D. Berkowitz, "Levels of Analysis Problems in International Studies," *International Interactions* 2, no. 3 (Summer 1986): 199–227.

8. For a good review of the development of U.S. operational planning for strategic operations from 1945 to 1960, see David Rosenberg, "Origins of Overkill," *International Security* 7, no. 4 (Spring 1983): 3–71.

9. V. D. Sokolovskii, *Military Strategy*, 3d ed., trans. Harriet Fast Scott (New York: Crane, Russak and Company, 1975).

10. The methodologies used to estimate the range of the Backfire were described to the authors in interviews with the participants.

11. The range for the Backfire is currently estimated at 8,000 kilometers when not refueled and flown at optimal speed and altitude. See U.S. Department of Defense, *Soviet Military Power, 1985* (Washington, D.C.: U.S. Government Printing Office, 1985), pp. 32–33; also see *The Military Balance, 1983–1984* (London: International Institute for Strategic Studies, 1983), p. 123.

12. Ewen Montagu, *The Man Who Never Was* (New York: Scholastic Book Services, 1953).

13. An account of the *Wolnosc i Niepodlenosc* appears in Thomas Powers, *The Man Who Kept the Secrets* (New York: Alfred A. Knopf, 1979), pp. 49–52.

14. Ogarkov has since been transferred, apparently to an operational command. For a general background on Soviet deception, see Viktor Suvorov, *Inside the Soviet Army* (New York: Macmillan, 1983), pp. 102–103. Soviet strategic deception has become a popular issue to raise for several Western writers, usually from the more conservative side of the political spectrum; see, for example, Richard Shultz and Roy Godson, *Disinformatsia: The Strategy of Soviet Deception* (New York: Pergamon Press, 1984).

15. U.S., Congress, Senate, Select Committee on Intelligence, *Meeting the Espionage Challenge: A Review of United States Counterintelligence and Security Programs* (Washington, D.C.: U.S. Government Printing Office, 1986), p. 142.

16. For example, see Sullivan, "Evaluating U.S. Intelligence Estimates," pp. 49–73.

17. Oleg Penkovskiy, *The Penkovskiy Papers* (New York: Avon Books, 1965), pp. 324–325; and Zhores A. Medvedev, *Soviet Science* (New York: W.W. Norton, 1978). Penkovskiy correctly reported the

basic cause of Nedelin's death—a missile explosion—but appears, from his memoirs, to have been mistaken in many of the details.

18. Numerous studies of the "missile gap" episode and the role of Soviet deception have been published; the best are probably Lawrence Freedman, *U.S. Intelligence and the Soviet Strategic Threat* (London: Macmillan, 1977); and John Prados, *The Soviet Estimate: U.S. Intelligence Analysis and the Russian Military Threat* (New York: Dial Press, 1982). Also see Edgar M. Bottome, *The Missile Gap* (Rutherford, N.J.: Farleigh Dickenson Press, 1971). A recent examination and its relevance to U.S. politics and the American space program appears in Walter A. McDougall, *The Heavens and the Earth* (New York: Basic Books, 1985), chap. 12.

19. Barton Whaley, *Covert German Rearmament, 1919–1939: Deception and Misperception* (Frederick, Md.: University Press of America, 1984), pp. 91–93. The Germans reported that the *Bismark* had a draft of 26 feet, 80,000 horsepower, 9-inch armor, and a flank speed of 27 knots; in truth, the figures were 34 feet, 150,000 horsepower, 16-inches, and 30 knots, respectively.

20. David C. Martin, *Wilderness of Mirrors* (New York: Harper and Row, 1980), pp. 198–206.

21. Stansfield Turner, *Secrecy and Democracy: The CIA in Transition* (New York: Houghton Mifflin, 1985), pp. 230–231.

22. Kenneth Arrow, *Social Choice and Individual Values* (New Haven, Conn.: Yale University Press, 1961).

23. James Gleick, *Chaos: Making a New Science* (New York: Viking Books, 1987). For a good summary of both the book and the problem, also see John Maddox "How Butterflies Cause Hurricanes," *New York Times Book Review*, October 25, 1987, p. 11.

24. See, for example, Morton H. Halperin, *Bureaucratic Politics and Foreign Policy* (Washington, D.C.: The Brookings Institution, 1974), pp. 134–172; Henry L. Britton, *International Relations in the Nuclear Age* (Albany, N.Y.: State University of New York Press, 1986), pp. 123–132; Robert D. Cantor, *Contemporary International Politics* (St. Paul, Minn.: West Publishing Company, 1986), pp. 332–365.

25. See the findings reported in Arthur S. Hulnick and Deborah Brammer, *The Impact of Intelligence on the Policy Review and Decision Process* (Washington, D.C.: Center for the Study of Intelligence, Central Intelligence Agency, January 1980).

26. Zbigniew Brzezinski, *Power and Principle* (New York: Farrar, Straus, Giroux, 1983), pp. 395–398; U.S., Congress, House, Permanent Select Committee on Intelligence, *Iran: Evaluation of U.S. Intelligence Performance Prior to November 1978* (Washington, D.C.:

U.S. Government Printing Office, 1979); Martin F. Herz, ed., *Contacts with the Opposition: A Symposium* (Washington, D.C.: Institute for the Study of Diplomacy, Georgetown University, 1979), p. 4; and Allan E. Goodman, "Reforming U.S. Intelligence," *Foreign Policy*, no. 67 (Summer 1987), pp. 121–136.

27. John Tower, Edmund Muskie, and Brent Scowcroft, *Report of the President's Special Review Board* (Washington, D.C.: U.S. Government Printing Office, February 26, 1987), pp. IV-2, IV-4. Also see Goodman, "Reforming U.S. Intelligence," pp. 121–136.

CHAPTER FIVE

1. Stansfield Turner, *Secrecy and Democracy: The CIA in Transition* (New York: Houghton Mifflin, 1985), p. 242.

2. The officials on the MAGIC distribution list were the Secretary of War, the Secretary of the Navy, the Chief of Staff of the Army, the Chief of Naval Operations, the Director of Military Intelligence, the Director of Naval Intelligence, the Chief of the Navy's War Plans Division, the Secretary of State, and the President's military aide. See Roberta Wohlstetter, *Pearl Harbor: Warning and Decision* (Stanford, Calif.: Stanford University Press, 1962), pp. 176–187; and Ronald Lewin, *The American Magic: Codes, Ciphers, and the Defeat of Japan* (New York: Farrar, Straus, Giroux, 1982), pp. 66–68.

3. Lewin, *The American Magic*, p. 67.

4. U.S., Congress, House, Permanent Select Committee on Intelligence, *A Compilation of Intelligence Laws and Related Laws and Executive Orders of Interest to the National Intelligence Community* (Washington, D.C.: U.S. Government Printing Office, July 1985), p. 7.

5. Turner, *Secrecy and Democracy*, pp. 254–257.

6. Bill Sweetman, *Stealth Aircraft: Secrets of Future Airpower* (Osceola, Wis.: Motorbooks International, 1986), pp. 14–30.

7. See Lewin, *The American Magic*, p. 19; and the Commission to Review DOD Security Policies and Practices (the "Stillwell Commission"), *Keeping the Nation's Secrets* (Washington, D.C.: Department of Defense, November 1985).

8. See Sherman Kent, *Strategic Intelligence for American World Policy* (Princeton, N.J.: Princeton University Press, 1949), chap. 6.

9. *Church Committee Report* 4: 13–14.

10. See Anthony Downs, *Inside Bureaucracy* (Boston: Little, Brown, 1962). *Church Committee Report* 4: 15–16.

11. No exact figure appears to be publicly available. According to

the *Church Committee Report* (vol. 4, p. 21), ORR alone had 461 personnel in July 1951. The Office of National Estimates never had more than 50 personnel, and this leaves OSI and the remnants of ORE (which eventually became the Office of Current Intelligence and the Office of Collection and Dissemination) unaccounted for. By 1953 ORR had grown to 766 persons, and the CIA's total analytical arm, which by then was informally designated the Directorate of Intelligence, included 3,338 personnel. It seems reasonable to assume that before the Korean War this figure was less than 900 but greater than 600.

12. *Church Committee Report* 4: 18.

13. Philip Taubman, "Casey and His CIA on the Rebound," *New York Times Magazine*, January 16, 1983, p. 35.

14. See *Director's Day Guide*, DRS-2600-926A-85 (Washington, D.C.: Defense Intelligence Agency, January 19, 1985), pp. 34-37.

15. This principle is consistent with the findings of investigations on collective choice in groups. See Kenneth Arrow, *Social Choice and Individual Values* (New Haven, Conn.: Yale University Press, 1961); and Amartya K. Sen, *Collective Choice and Social Welfare* (San Francisco: Holden-Day, 1970).

16. The following account is based on interviews with former intelligence officials, including most of the key participants.

17. Interviews. Also see Daniel O. Graham, "The Intelligence Mythology of Washington," *Strategic Review* 4, no. 3 (Summer 1976): 59-66.

18. Bruce D. Berkowitz, "Intelligence in the Organizational Context," *Orbis* 29, no. 3 (Fall 1985): 571-596.

19. See Edgar M. Bottome, *The Missile Gap* (Rutherford, N.J.: Farleigh Dickenson Press, 1971), for the political impact of the early underestimates; and Lawrence Freedman, *U.S. Intelligence and the Soviet Strategic Threat* (London: Macmillan, 1977), for a good study of the later underestimates and their political repercussions.

20. Albert Wohlstetter, "Legends of the Strategic Arms Race," USSI Report 75-1 (Washington, D.C.: United States Strategic Institute, 1975).

CHAPTER SIX

1. *Congressional Record* (September 24, 1986), p. S13564.

2. See Stansfield Turner, *Secrecy and Democracy: The CIA in Transi-*

tion (New York: Houghton Mifflin, 1985), p. 88. For the origins of Civil Air Transport, Air America, and other CIA proprietary air transport activities, see Victor Marchetti and John Marks, *The CIA and the Cult of Intelligence* (New York: Alfred A. Knopf, 1974), pp. 137–149. For the former linkages between Radio Free Europe and Radio Liberty and the CIA, see Marchetti and Marks, *The CIA and the Cult of Intelligence*, pp. 167–170. A good summary of CIA proprietaries in the early phases of the Indochina conflict appears in John Prados, *The Sky Would Fall* (New York: Dial Press, 1983).

3. See the Statement of Hon. William Proxmire in U.S., Congress, Senate, *Whether Disclosure of Funds Authorized for Intelligence Activities is in the Public Interest*, Hearings before the U.S. Select Committee on Intelligence (April 1977), pp. 31–33. (Proxmire cites Colby and offers a contrary argument of his own.)

4. Testimony of William Colby, in ibid., p. 48.

5. Estimating Soviet defense spending is one of the most enduring controversies among intelligence analysts. The problem lies in determining how much of the activity of civilian ministries is dedicated to defense. For some examples of controversy, see *A Dollar Cost Comparison of Soviet and U.S. Defense Activities*, SR 77–10001U (Washington, D.C.: Central Intelligence Agency, 1977); William T. Lee, *The Estimation of Soviet Defense Expenditures for 1955–1975: An Unconventional Approach* (New York: Praeger, 1977); Steven Rosefielde, *False Science: Underestimating the Soviet Arms Buildup* (New Brunswick, N.J.: Transaction Books, 1982).

6. For a brief overview of relations between academe and the CIA, see Robert M. Gates, "The CIA and the University," speech at the John F. Kennedy School of Government, Harvard University, February 13, 1986.

7. See Robin W. Winks, *Cloak and Gown: Scholars in the Secret Wars, 1939–1961* (New York: William Morrow, 1987); and Bradley F. Smith, *The Shadow Warriors: OSS and the Origins of the CIA* (New York: Basic Books, 1983), pp. 360–389.

8. For an illustration of the CIA's difficulties in meeting its requirements for Indochina experts (and a humorous account of how at least one of these specialists was recruited), see Frank Snepp, *Decent Interval* (New York: Random House, 1977), pp. 18–19. For an account of some of the problems the surfeit of Indochina experts posed in the last half of the 1970s, see Turner, *Secrecy and Democracy*, pp. 197–198.

9. U.S., Congress, Senate, Committee on Governmental Affairs,

Permanent Subcommittee on Investigations, *Federal Government Security Clearance Programs* (Washington, D.C.: U.S. Government Printing Office, 1985), p. 287.

10. Max Weber, "Bureaucracy," in *From Max Weber: Essays in Sociology*, trans. H. H. Gerth and C. Wright Mills (New York: Oxford University Press, 1962), pp. 196–244. Also see Anthony Downs, *Inside Bureaucracy* (Boston: Little, Brown, 1967).

11. Turner, *Secrecy and Democracy*, pp. 224–226.

CHAPTER SEVEN

1. Statement by Robert M. Gates, in "Nomination of Robert M. Gates," hearing before the Select Committee on Intelligence of the United States Senate (Washington, D.C.: U.S. Government Printing Office, April 10, 1986), p. 39. For a discussion of how intelligence has ostensively benefited from oversight, see David Gries, "The CIA and Congress: Uneasy Partners," *Studies in Intelligence* (Autumn 1987), pp. 77–84.

2. See, for example, the comments of Richard Russell and John Stennis, as cited by Thomas Powers, *The Man Who Kept the Secrets* (New York: Alfred A. Knopf, 1979), pp. 354–355. Russell was reported to have told the DCI that there were some matters that he just as soon did not want to know. Stennis was quoted as saying that, in some cases, "you had to make up your mind that you are going to have an intelligence agency and protect it as such, and shut your eyes some and take what is coming."

APPENDIX A

1. Dan Morgan, *Merchants of Grain* (New York: Viking Press, 1979), pp. 50–51.

2. William T. Lee, *The Estimation of Soviet Defense Expenditures for 1955–1975: An Unconventional Approach* (New York: Praeger, 1977). Also see Donald F. Burton, "Estimating Soviet Defense Spending," *Problems of Communism* 32, no. 2 (March-April 1983).

3. See also Richard Helms, "Remarks At a Donovan Award Dinner," Delivered to Association of Former Intelligence Officers, May 24, 1983. Also see William Stevenson, *Intrepid's Last Case* (New York: Ballentine, 1983), chap. 1.

4. Laqueur, *A World of Secrets: the Uses and Limits of Intelligence* (New York: Basic Books, 1985), p. 226.

5. Richard Bissell interview, in John Ranelagh, *The Agency: The Rise and Decline of the CIA* (New York: Simon and Schuster, 1986), p. 325. Also see Leonard Mosely, *Dulles: A Biography of Eleanor, Allen, and John Foster Dulles and Their Family Network* (New York: Dial Press, 1978), p. 432.

6. An up-to-date summary of these and other recent espionage cases appears in U.S., Congress, Senate, Select Committee on Intelligence, *Meeting the Espionage Challenge* (Washington, D.C.: U.S. Government Printing Office, 1986).

7. Comments by Deputy Assistant Secretary of Defense Gaffney, cited by Walter Andres, "U.S. Policy on Spy Satellites Risky, Pentagon Official Says," *Washington Times*, May 14, 1986, p. 4.

8. For President Eisenhower's restrictions on u-2 flights over the Soviet Union, see Stephen E. Ambrose, *Eisenhower the President* (New York: Simon and Schuster, 1984), pp. 513–515. President Kennedy halted u-2 flights over Cuba during the Missile Crisis following the downing of a u-2 over China; Kennedy feared such an incident would further raise tensions. See Graham T. Allison, *Essence of Decision* (Boston: Little, Brown, 1971), pp. 120–122.

9. John Prados, *The Soviet Estimate: U.S. Intelligence Analysis and the Russian Military Threat* (New York: Dial Press, 1982), p. 98.

10. Richard K. Betts, "Surprise Despite Warning: Why Sudden Attacks Succeed," *Political Science Quarterly* 95, no. 4 (Winter 1980–1981): 565; and Jon McLin, *NATO and the Czechoslovakian Crisis, Part II: Invasion, Reaction, and Stocktaking*, American Universities Field Staff Reports, Western Europe Series, vol. 4, no. 4 (Hanover, N.H.: American Universities Field Staff, February 1969), p. 6. For a description of the intelligence community's response to the KAL 007 incident, see Seymour Hersh, *The Target is Destroyed* (New York: Vantage Press, 1986).

11. Viktor Suvorov, *Inside the Soviet Army* (New York: Macmillan, 1983), p. 106.

12. Henry A. Kissinger, *Years of Upheaval* (New York: Harper and Row, 1982), pp. 225–226, 461–462. Also see Ranelagh, *The Agency*, pp. 580–583.

13. Central Intelligence Agency, *The Military Buildup in Cuba*, SNIE 85-3-62 (declassified).

14. Betts, "Surprise Despite Warning."

15. Peter Wydon, *Bay of Pigs: The Untold Story* (London: Jonathan Cape, 1979).

16. *Iran: Evaluation of U.S. Intelligence Performance Prior to November 1978*, staff report, U.S., Congress, House, Subcommittee on Evaluation, Permanent Subcommittee on Intelligence (Washington, D.C.: U.S. Government Printing Office, 1979), pp. 4–5.

Index

INDEX